Lord of the Flies

WILLIAM GOLDING

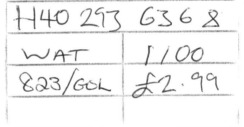
Guide written by

Stewart Martin

A *Letts* EXPLORE Literature Guide

Extracts from *Lord of the Flies* by William Golding are reprinted by kind permission of Faber and Faber Limited.

Examination questions produced by kind permission of the Northern Examination and Assessment Board. The suggested answers supplied to the Exam Board questions are solely the responsibility of the author and are not supplied or approved by the Exam Board.

First published 1994
Reprinted 1994 twice, 1995, 1996, 1997, 1998
This edition edited by Ron Simpson

Letts Educational
Aldine House
Aldine Place
London W12 8AW
0181 740 2266

Text © John Mahoney and Stewart Martin 1994

Typeset by Jordan Publishing Design

Self-test questions devised by Hilary Lissenden

Text design Jonathan Barnard

Cover and text illustrations Hugh Marsha"

Design © BPP (Letts Educational) Ltd

British Library Cataloguing in Publicat
A CIP record for this book is available from

ISBN 1 85758 263 2

Printed and bound in Great Britain by

Letts Educational is the trading name of BP

■ Contents

■ Plot synopsis

Lord of the Flies is set on an imaginary, remote tropical island. A plane has crashed whilst evacuating children from a war-torn country. A group of boys are the only survivors: the members of a church choir and their leader, Jack Merridew, Ralph, a fat, short-sighted boy nicknamed Piggy, and a number of other boys of various ages.

Ralph and Piggy discover a conch shell and when Ralph blows it all the survivors gather on the beach. Ralph is elected leader of the group, but allows Jack to remain leader of the choir, who are to be hunters. Ralph, Jack and Simon (one of the choir) explore the island and find it uninhabited.

The conch is used to control meetings by giving whoever holds it the right to speak. Some of the smaller children are frightened by a 'beastie' they think they have seen in the jungle at night, but the older boys dismiss this idea. Ralph says they need shelters on the beach and a signal fire on the mountain. Jack volunteers the hunters to keep the fire burning.

Jack learns to hunt the pigs on the island, whilst Ralph and a few others build a few rickety shelters. A ship's smoke is seen on the horizon but the signal fire has gone out because the choir is hunting. The ship passes. The hunters return with a killed pig and there is a tense confrontation between the two groups about the fire being out.

At night a dead pilot parachutes onto the mountain after a battle high above the island. When the dead pilot is discovered, terror spreads amongst the boys, who think it is 'the beast'. Following an unsuccessful challenge for the leadership, Jack sets up his own 'tribe'. Jack's tribe hunts and kills a pig and leaves its head as an offering for the beast. Simon falls into a fit, in which he has a 'conversation' with the dead pig's head, then faints.

When he recovers, Simon climbs the mountain alone and sees 'the beast' for what it is. Jack's tribe holds a great feast and performs a ritual dance, during which Simon returns. He is attacked and killed as 'the beast' by the dancing, chanting boys.

Ralph's small group tries to keep the signal fire alight. Jack's tribe attacks and steals Piggy's glasses to make fire with. Ralph's group goes to demand Piggy's glasses back, taking the conch with them.

During the confrontation with Jack's tribe, Piggy is killed and the conch smashed. Ralph escapes, but the rest of his group are captured. Jack's tribe hunts Ralph, intending to kill him and, during the hunt, sets fire to the island. A naval officer, whose ship has been attracted by the smoke, rescues them.

About William Golding

William Golding was born in Cornwall in 1911. His father was a schoolteacher and his mother was active in the women's suffrage movement. He went to Marlborough Grammar School and then to Oxford University. His parents had always encouraged him to study the sciences, but in his second year at Oxford he changed to a study of literature.

Golding became a teacher after leaving university, but with the outbreak of the Second World War he joined the Royal Navy and eventually became commander of a ship. During these war years he saw much action, including the sinking of the *Bismarck* and the D-Day Normandy landings. The impact of these wartime experiences influenced his outlook, as can be seen by his later writing. He said that much of what he saw in war could not be accounted for, 'except on the basis of original evil'.

In 1945 he returned to teaching English at Bishop Wordsworth's School in Salisbury. He remained there until 1962. During this time he established himself as a writer. With the publication of *Lord of the Flies*, he was hailed as an outstanding new novelist.

In Golding's book of collected essays, *The Hot Gates*, there is a piece about *Lord of the Flies*, called 'Fable', in which he says, 'Before the Second World War I believed in the perfectibility of social man; that a correct structure of society would produce goodwill; and that therefore you could remove all social ills by a reorganisation of society. It is possible that today I believe something of the same again; but after the war I did not because I was unable to. I had discovered what one man could do to another.'

Much of Golding's work illustrates his pessimism about man's nature and fate. *Lord of the Flies* reflects his considerations of these concepts after many years of close observation of the boys he had taught and seen develop. William Golding could not be described as a prolific novelist, but after *Lord of the Flies* he produced several other highly-rated novels which tend to explore themes of sin, mysticism and physical and/or moral isolation. For instance, *The Spire* (1964), set in the Middle Ages, deals with a cathedral dean's crazed attempts to build a spire on his cathedral, whilst *Pincher Martin* (1956) is about the experiences of an apparently drowned sailor.

Golding married in 1939, had two children, and lived in Wiltshire. In 1983 he received the distinguished award, the Nobel Prize for Literature. He died in 1993.

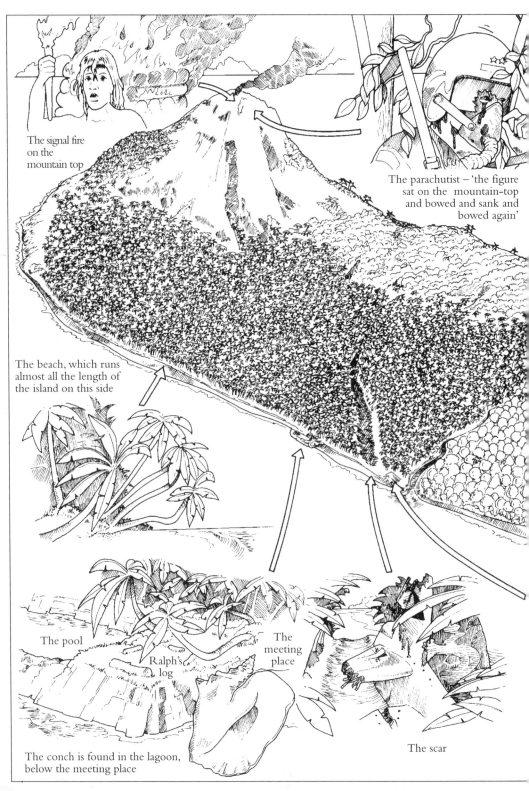

The signal fire on the mountain top

The parachutist – 'the figure sat on the mountain-top and bowed and sank and bowed again'

The beach, which runs almost all the length of the island on this side

The pool

Ralph's log

The meeting place

The scar

The conch is found in the lagoon, below the meeting place

The Island

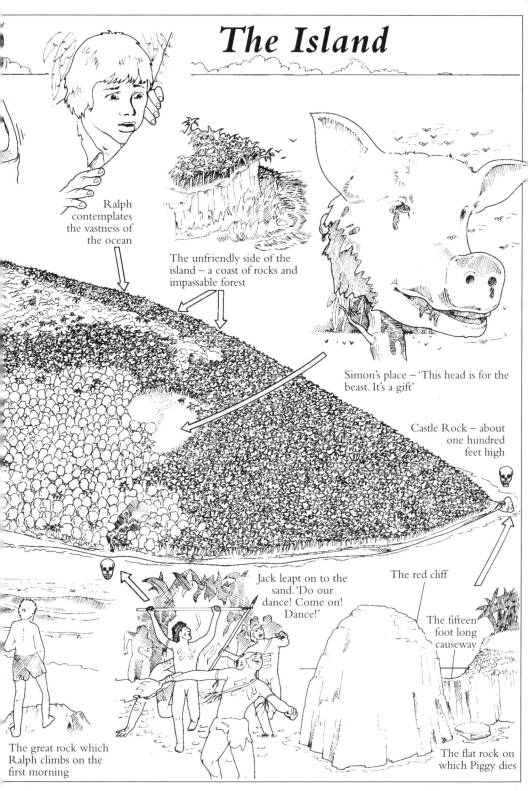

Ralph contemplates the vastness of the ocean

The unfriendly side of the island – a coast of rocks and impassable forest

Simon's place – 'This head is for the beast. It's a gift'

Castle Rock – about one hundred feet high

The great rock which Ralph climbs on the first morning

Jack leapt on to the sand. 'Do our dance! Come on! Dance!'

The red cliff

The fifteen foot long causeway

The flat rock on which Piggy dies

■ Who's who in *Lord of the Flies*

u - important

Ralph

Ralph

Ralph's character develops as the novel progresses. Unlike Jack, he becomes more aware of the inner nature of humankind. He is, at the beginning, a happy yet sensitive and responsible person who eventually comes to understand the 'darkness of man's heart'. He demonstrates courage, authority, compassion and respect for civilised values. These moral standards are crushed in a world which is run by Jack's kind of rules. Ralph's failure to lead a democratic society successfully symbolises the failure of humankind to recognise or deal with the force of evil within itself.

Piggy

Piggy

Piggy's physical appearance, his common sense and scientific, intellectual point of view make him the only adult-type figure on the island. He continually shatters the boys' illusions and interrupts their desire to play. When the 'play' develops into something much more sinister, he is killed because he spoils 'the game'. By then, the game has become a terrible reality, a war between good and evil.

Jack

Jack

Jack is a leader but his methods are the natural opposite to those of Ralph. Jack is dictatorial and aggressive; he has a strong desire to lead and asserts himself through his prowess as a hunter, which deteriorates into lust for killing. The character of Jack shows how, without the restrictions of adults or society, certain people revert to primitive desires and actions. Jack's character changes as the story unfolds, but this change is one of degeneration. At the start he asserts his superiority through his background, but he is irresponsible and needs his rewards straight away. He has no patience with constructive, positive things, which is why he grows tired of debates and hut building. His love of hunting stems from the sense of power killing gives him. He abuses his power as a leader, and his freedom from social restraints unleashes the evil latent within his character.

Roger

Roger does not so much develop as a character as reveal his nature through the course of the book. He represents the merciless type of killer and torturer whose sadistic tendencies are let loose on society if dictators take control. Characters like Roger are not leaders, but help to make tyrannical leaders stronger.

Simon

Simon represents the mystic; he has vision and intuition and is the saint or Christ-like figure who has compassion for his fellows. Like many mystics, he fails to communicate his insight to others.

Often mystics enter 'trances' to find the truth they are seeking. Simon is subject to faints and hallucinations and his fits symbolise the visionary experience. His conversation with the Lord of the Flies (the dead pig's head) crystallises Golding's message, which is that evil is within everyone. Every individual must wrestle with 'the beast' within, and either accept and be ruled by it, or conquer and reject it. Simon's response is to continue with his quest for truth. He is rejected as 'batty' and slaughtered in a ritual frenzy. He represents the martyr who is neither valued nor understood by his society.

Littluns

The littluns represent ordinary people who follow leaders without too much thought as to why they do so. These very young boys are helpless and act as examples of humankind's carelessness towards the weak and needy. Separated from adult care, the littluns gather food, play in daylight and suffer nightmares. They introduce the beast of fear to the boys' community.

◼ Themes and images in
Lord of the Flies

Themes are the important ideas that run through the book. You will come across them lots of times. They connect together the story, the characters and the different scenes in the book.

When words and descriptions suggest a picture in your mind, that is called an **image**. Images are often used to make an idea stronger, or to encourage you to think of things from a particular point of view. If you described someone as being 'as thin as a rake' or as behaving 'like a wild animal', you would be using simple images.

The themes and images below are not an exhaustive list because the novel is a rich source of imagery, symbolism and 'meaning'. Some interesting themes have been omitted altogether, like the use Golding makes of references to the ocean's tide. What follows is a starting-point only – do not be afraid to use your own interpretations and sensitivity in your reading.

Background to the themes

Lord of the Flies is an **allegory**. This means a narrative which works on two levels of meaning: the literal story level and the moral, spiritual or religious level. For example, some critics have seen the boys' life on the island as a parallel to the rise of Hitler and fascism in Germany before the Second World War. While it is probable that Golding had this in mind when he wrote the book, the plot is also relevant to the general rise of dictatorships in contemporary times and throughout history all over the world. The references to other children's 'Island Adventure' stories create an ironic parallel with the boys' experience in *Lord of the Flies*. *The Coral Island* (by R M Ballantyne), which was one of Golding's sources, depicts a group of English boys who maintain civilised principles on their island, and even convert a group of savages to Christianity! This is the type of 'show' the naval officer expects 'a pack of British boys' to have put up.

In *Lord of the Flies*, Golding makes powerful use of the literary traditions of myth and fable. A **myth** is an ancient traditional story of gods and heroes. The island setting enables Golding to draw a parallel with the Garden of Eden, which was a place of innocence until the gaining of knowledge led to humankind's expulsion. Images like the snake can be recognised in this context. Other biblical parallels appear through the character of Simon. The story explores the Christian idea that evil is inherent in people, by asking the reader to accept the concept of original sin. A **fable** is rather like a myth in some ways, except that it is clearly a story which is intended to instruct. It is a tale with a moral. Golding described a fable as a story with 'a human lesson tucked away in it'. The lesson tucked away in *Lord of the Flies* is that people are not naturally good when freed from the restraints of society. Evil is shown as an awesome force which must be recognised, so that it can be controlled. As you read the novel, ask yourself whether you accept this view.

Golding uses the **imagery and language** of the novel to help him get across what he has in mind. For example, the boys' language is **colloquial**, that is, believable and normal for boys of that age range. **Slang** is used throughout their speech and arguments – some of it will sound out of date now, but remember that this novel was first published in 1954. However, a boy's ability to speak and convince (for example, Ralph's eloquence) does not necessarily mean that his ideas are clear. This also works the other way around: Piggy has the clearest ideas on the island, but the worst grammar; and Simon sees the darkness (the beast) in the soul of humankind more clearly than anybody else, but cannot persuade the others to listen to him. Images using **colour** are used carefully throughout the novel. Colour often helps to make a link between the natural surroundings and the boys, and it is sometimes symbolic – like the colour of Jack's hair, the colours of the mask and the choir's uniform, and the colour of the conch at the start and then at the end of the novel.

The beast

The beast

The beast represents the way in which people make something outside of themselves evil, so that they can maintain an image of themselves as good. This allows them to avoid the responsibility of looking carefully inside themselves – it allows them to avoid self-knowledge.

Golding uses the boys' imagination, daydreams and nightmares to show us their fears and desires. These things illuminate the sense of loss in the children, and their need for security. The snakes are only present on the island in the boys' imaginations. The snake image is traditionally symbolic of evil and is appropriate for Golding's argument that evil comes from within. The beast gives the boys' fear something to focus on. There are several kinds of fear depicted in the novel, apart from the obvious physical fear of the trapped piglet at the start and (in a different sense) the trapped Ralph at the end. Fear is often, although not always, associated with guilt. There is the fear of the truth, as when the boys do not at first want to accept that they may never be rescued. Later, some of them do not want to accept that they killed Simon. There is the spiritual fear of the beast that is themselves, which is why they will not listen to Simon.

The arrival of the dead parachutist gives a physical form to the beast. In reality he is a pathetic figure, killed in war and robbed of all human dignity in death. The moving, decomposing corpse is macabre, but there is nothing supernatural about it. It takes its place in nature, along with the flies that feast on it, and is finally claimed by the sea.

Defects exist in any human society and they are usually caused by defects in human nature – what Golding sees as the existing but undeveloped evil in humankind. This is the beast. What happens in the novel is an example of how, in the right set of circumstances, the beast will reveal itself and bring about corruption.

The conch

The conch

The conch is a beautiful object, a part of the natural world which is untouched and unspoilt by people. It becomes a symbol of authority, common sense and democratic discipline. Its destruction symbolises the wilful destruction of order and rational behaviour. The conch in Greek mythology was used by the sea god Triton to calm or raise the oceans. Notice as you read the novel which characters respect the conch, which ones simply obey it and which ones challenge and finally disregard its authority. The boys gradually lose their innocence in the novel – echoed by the way the conch loses its colour.

Darkness and death

Darkness and death

Darkness in the novel is both a time of fear and a symbol of evil and degradation. The darkness can be literal, as with the darkness of the jungle and of night, and in this form it starts off as harmless and natural. Darkness becomes more spiritual with the mention of the beast. From this point on, the natural darkness of night gradually becomes the superstitious 'darkness' of ignorance and fear. Eventually it becomes 'the darkness of man's heart'.

Light symbolises freedom from ignorance. The riotous colours and fierce light of day are contrasted with the loss of security that darkness brings.

There are three certain human deaths on the island. The first is of a littlun, by accident; the second is of Simon, by crazed excitement; and the third is of Piggy, by savage murder. These deaths, and the different reasons for them, symbolise the boys' degeneration. The deaths of the pigs chart the hunters' movement towards total savagery. Initially, the hunters are unable to kill a piglet. You should also consider death in the novel within the context of the atomic bomb and the dead pilot who drops on to the island.

Nature

Nature

Golding sets his novel on an unspoiled island, which effectively isolates his characters from the world. He creates a microcosm (a mini-world) and by making us look closely at the nature of this microcosm, he makes us consider the real, 'whole' world and the condition of humankind.

The sea represents the vast distance between the boys and the civilisation from which they are cut off. The contrast between the sea on one side of the island and the sea on the other side, echoes the division between the two groups of boys. Similarly, the storm creates a background to the increasing tension and exploding violence in the boys' experience. Showing nature in sympathy with the moods and feelings of man is a common device in literature. It is sometimes known as the 'pathetic fallacy', which is the crediting of nature or inanimate objects with human emotions.

Golding's descriptions of the vegetation and natural life on the island work on two levels: they reinforce mood and reflect the continuing beauty in nature. Nature is shown as balanced and unified, in contrast with the divisions appearing amongst the boys. For example, food is a natural resource of the island but has painful repercussions: fruit gives the boys diarrhoea and pig meat comes to symbolise power. Interestingly, the boys make little use of the sea as a source of food.

Images of heat are also frequent. Heat is the first force to change the boys' usual behaviour. It appears in two different forms: natural heat, like the temperature of the island, and the heat of fire. These are often used to emphasise the emotional, 'primeval' heat in certain characters.

Order

Order

The concern of some of the boys with rules and order echoes a basic requirement for civilisation. Civilisation is culture which has advanced beyond the primitive and savage. At first the boys are products of civilised culture; at the end they are degenerate remnants of a small, isolated group, which has stripped itself of the refinements of moral values.

The assembly is the boys' attempt at a democratically organised form of government. It begins well, but the presence of two natural leaders causes a split in the power structure of the boys' society and leads to its break-up. The conch is the assembly's symbol of authority. The attempt to organise a democratic society, where each member has a voice, fails when Jack's regime emerges as a dictatorship. Responsibility is a quality necessary for good leadership in a civilised society. It is displayed by Ralph, but discarded by Jack.

The problem of order and its relationship to leadership is a major area of conflict in the boys' situation. Both Jack and Ralph are 'leader-types'. The conflict arises because of their differing methods and morals. When the title 'chief' is adopted by Jack it indicates a change in emphasis from the leadership of Ralph. The trappings of being chief include position and respect – like they did for Ralph – but Jack's style of leadership also commands fear and obedience. Physique plays an important part in the way the boys see themselves and their credibility within the group. Notice that the two leaders are the biggest, strongest boys on the island.

At the start of the novel, fire is used for the common good – to attract rescuers. Fire has always been seen as an important aspect of order and security – we often think of the discovery of fire as a great step out of savagery towards civilisation. But fire also holds the power to devastate and kill. Golding's symbolism makes us aware of the way all things have good and bad sides to them, and underlines a major theme of the book: the presence of both good and evil in everyone.

The use of reason is a powerful quality of the human mind. Once the ordering power of reason is lost, the worst aspects of human nature take over. Reason appears in two forms – firstly as Piggy's common sense. Common sense is valued in civilised society, but it is undervalued on the island because it tends to spoil the 'fun'. Secondly, reason appears as knowledge. Knowledge on the island takes three forms: that which has already been learned (represented by Piggy), unlearned knowledge born of intuition (represented by Simon) and knowledge gained through loss of innocence (experienced by Ralph).

Piggy's glasses are the main symbol of survival, because they are essential for fire-making. But they also symbolise reason, the ability to see clearly, and man's inhumanity to man (as when they are broken and then stolen). Throughout the novel the fate of the glasses illustrates the loss of reasonable behaviour. The breaking of the glasses coincides with the abandonment of civilised values. In the end they become a 'talisman' – evidence of Jack's tyrannical leadership.

War is depicted as a result of the loss of reason and as an inherent part of humankind's condition. War has brought about the boys' situation, and the result is war between the two groups. The boys will return at the end not to stability, but war. The naval officer who rescues them represents adult authority and civilised British values. But the images surrounding his arrival also reflect war, and have ominous undertones.

Savagery

Savagery

Play and 'fun' result from the boys' pleasure in having their own island. It is a daytime escape from night-time fears for the littluns. For the older boys, play is distorted into a sinister, devilish activity. Fun develops into irresponsibility, then into torture and murder. Notice, for example, how 'trundling' rocks provides an innocent pastime at first, but in the end, rocks are deadly weapons.

One of the movements traceable through the novel is in the choir, who change to hunters, to a tribe, to savages. This downward path is sometimes known as atavism. Each experience of killing changes the boys and widens the gap between the hunters and those who cling to civilised values. The boys eventually descend to a primitive level of savagery ruled by an arrogant chief. At this stage they are no longer recognisable, physically or mentally, as the boys described at the start of the novel. Golding leaves us to imagine what kind of adults they might become after their experiences on the island. The first clear sign of the emergence of the savage is the mask. At first the mask is intended as camouflage, but it generates a strange and primitive freedom in the wearer. The mask contributes to the degeneration of the tribe. 'Tribe' is the word used by Jack to describe his band of followers. At first the word suggests an element of play, but the tribe quickly develops into a savage band of killers.

Rituals offer security and reassurance and make events feel more important and permanent for us, whether these are the rituals of joining a gang, of a marriage service, or those of the church. Ritual emerges as a powerful force on the island. Through rituals of chant, dance and superstition, the tribe is held together and commits atrocities. The chant of the hunters is a ritual which is repeated, growing in fierceness on each occasion. The most extreme violence of the chant coincides with the breaking of the last barriers of civilised behaviour, when Simon is murdered.

One way of looking at this novel is to consider it as being structured upon six hunts. Each successful hunt brings the boys closer to the savage side of human nature. The pig is the object of the hunt, as a source of food. But the pig-hunt becomes a symbol of the decline of civilised values and the loss of innocence. As 'Lord of the Flies', the sow's head illustrates the superstitious, ritualistic level to which the tribe of hunters has sunk.

Examiners' tips

This icon is used to draw attention to sections of the **Text commentary** that are particularly relevant to the titles considered in **How to write an examination Essay**. Each time it is used, a note provides a comment or piece of advice.

■ Text commentary

Chapter 1

A plane has crashed on a remote, jungle-like island. All the survivors are boys. The first survivors we meet are Ralph, who is athletic and good-looking, and Piggy, who is fat, short-sighted and asthmatic. They seem to have little in common except a concern to locate and organise other survivors. The boys find a large conch shell and when Piggy explains to Ralph how to blow it, its loud trumpeting summons boys from all directions.

Amongst the boys attracted by the noise of the conch is Jack Merridew, who leads his choir with arrogance and military precision. Only when one of the choir (Simon) faints from standing in the heat does he allow them to relax. He asserts his authority but is disappointed when a general vote elects Ralph as leader. Ralph offers Jack leadership of his choir as hunters.

Ralph, Jack and Simon explore the island and find it uninhabited. They are enchanted by the beauty and freedom the island offers and claim it as their own. They find a trapped piglet but Jack, who has a knife, cannot bring himself to kill it.

We meet Piggy and Ralph

Piggy

Piggy is physically disadvantaged: he is short, fat, very short-sighted, and suffers from asthma. He can't run and he can't swim. Look out for evidence of this. Can you identify Piggy as a particular 'type' of boy?

Ralph, in contrast, is tall, fair, agile, a good swimmer with a 'mildness about his mouth and eyes that proclaimed no devil'. This gives a clear indication of Ralph's character. Golding saw him as 'the average, rather more than average, man of goodwill and common sense; the man who makes mistakes because he simply does not understand at first the nature of the disease from which they all suffer.'

Ralph

Life on the island

Nature

Notice that it is the heat which is the first force to create a change in the boys' usual behaviour. Compare this happy picture of nakedness with the concern for appearance which the boys later have in Chapter 11.

Notice how the fruit gives the boys diarrhoea. This is the first hint that their Garden of Eden may not be as perfect as it at first seems.

Piggy doesn't care what they call him – so long as it isn't 'Piggy'

The nickname 'Piggy' firmly establishes the way his peers see him – his 'type'.

Piggy

Notice the irony that, in the novel itself, the pig is first of all a beast, then a ritual offering to the beast, then Lord of the Flies; at the same time the name 'Piggy' is used for the most rational person in the group.

Piggy is the character in the novel about whom we change our minds the most, although he himself does not change at all. One of Piggy's characteristics is his consistency, as shown in his friendship (for Ralph). Piggy does not seem to change his mind much. Why do you think this is so?

It is ironical that Piggy possesses so many of the qualities needed for a leader in this situation (logic, reason, understanding of organisation and the group), yet is totally unsuitable for the role of Chief because of other qualities of character and background. See how far these contradictions are revealed at the outset and consider what Piggy's actual role is (or should be) on the island.

Ralph as he is at the beginning

Ralph

At the start, Ralph is a fun-loving boy, excited by the prospect of adventure without the restrictions of grown-up authority. We see many events through his eyes and are given many insights into the way he feels about events and people. Does Golding do this with any other character? (Look at Chapter 9.)

Piggy asks how Ralph's father knows the boys are on the island

Piggy is a realist. He explains that they need to face the fact that no one knows their location, and that they must organise themselves. Compare this reaction with Ralph's early pleasure at being on a beautiful island. In many ways, Ralph is a typical product of the British middle class. His father is a naval commander and Ralph apparently has a happy family background. However, his dream in Chapter 7 suggests that his mother is dead or his parents are divorced and he sees less than he would like of his father. He represents the model son, a good boy with a sense of the importance of democracy, but at the same time fun-loving and easy-going.

Two views of the world

Golding said that he remembered discussions with his own scientifically minded father, and Piggy represents this kind of approach to the world. By contrast, Golding was a believer in the supernatural. This coloured the way he reacted to his wartime experiences; he saw Nazism as an evil force, not just the product of a corrupt political system.

The conch is found

Piggy has acquired valuable knowledge and information during his life. He recognises the value of the conch. Although Ralph finds the conch in the lagoon and is attracted by its beauty, it is Piggy who advises of its practical use to make a loud noise which will attract other survivors.

The conch is blown seven times in *Lord of the Flies*. Look at each one in turn. When does blowing the conch lead to stirring things up, and when does it lead to quietening them down? The first time the conch is blown, it heralds the birth of civilised order on the island. Contrast this with what happens when the conch is blown for the last time. Why do you think Ralph does not blow the conch when he calls the meeting in Chapter 4?

The conch

'We can use this to call the others. Have a meeting. They'll come when they hear us.' To begin with the conch is simply a convenient noise-maker. Think of the symbolism that later surrounds it and how the boys' attitude to it reveals their characters and the existence/collapse of democracy.

Jack appears with the choir

Jack collects the choir around him. They wear a black uniform. The military

discipline of the choir is more striking than its religious character. This is ominous. Some critics have seen Jack as a representation of Hitler, and the choir as an image for the Nazis. It is possible that Golding had this in his mind, but he could just as easily have had in mind the type of people who

Jack

have become powerful forces in society in the past, and who continue to do so. Such people usually begin as dedicated revolutionaries, and form tight-knit groups under strong leadership. But they often impose their values upon others by means of force and become corrupt and vicious tyrants.

The character of Jack

Even though he has been in a catastrophic air crash, and is now on an island

very different from the one he left, Jack carries on as leader of the choir and treats the choristers strictly. At Jack's first appearance in the novel, we recognise him as a natural leader. Which words and phrases suggest his authority, determination and power?

Jack

Jack wears the uniform of the head chorister. Later, he and his choristers change to another kind of 'uniform' – one of painted faces and masks. Notice the colour of the choristers' cloaks. Black and red are traditionally associated with evil, magic, the devil and hell-fire, and are connected with Jack throughout the novel. The colours he later paints on the mask are red, white and black, and he has red hair. At one level, Jack's red hair suggests a short and fiery temper. At another level, Jack's connections with the colour red suggest blood, or hell and the devil. Contrast these suggestions with Golding's description of Ralph's appearance – especially his eyes.

There are Christian symbols, crosses, on the choir's uniform, but look at Golding's first introduction of it: 'something dark was fumbling along'. If you wish to write about the transformation in Jack and the choir, note that it first appears as a dark creature (beast?); an important event for many essay titles.

Jack as a leader of others

Jack

Jack is ruthless towards his group. The boys are exhausted and Simon faints. What does this tell us about the kind of leader Jack is?

Jack does not want to be known by his first name. What does this tell you about his character? What is Jack called by the end of the book?

Ralph tells the others about Piggy's name

Piggy needs to be accepted by the others, but is vulnerable to their mockery.

Roger

Notice his reaction to their teasing about his nickname. How does Ralph react? What can you learn of Ralph's character from this?

When the laughter dies away we meet Roger, a 'slight, furtive boy'. At this stage his character is unrevealed and he is something of a mystery.

' "I ought to be chief," said Jack...'

Jack feels he has a natural right to be the leader. Golding says he has

Ralph

'arrogance'. Why do you think Ralph feels the need to compromise, to 'offer something'? Would you agree that those personal characteristics which caused Ralph to be elected as leader are the same ones which make his leadership ineffective as the story progresses?

Decision-making is an important part of government. Notice Ralph's need to have time to think – he says 'I can't decide what to do straight off.' Do you think this weakens Ralph's leadership?

Simon and Piggy see things differently to the other boys

Simon

Simon is described as a 'skinny, vivid little boy', who is prone to fainting. Is there any hint in Chapter 1 that he sees things differently from the other boys?

Because of his physique, Piggy is made an 'outsider', and is excluded from the group of explorers. Can you think of a reason why he should, by rights, have been included?

The island

A major feature of the island is the mountain. Many mountains feature

Nature

significantly in the Bible (for example, when Moses receives the Law of God and the Ten Commandments) and in many parts of the world mountains are holy places. But mountains have to be climbed to find the truth. At first the boys climb the mountain to discover the truth of their whereabouts. Later, Simon climbs the mountain to find out the truth about the beast: it is only a dead man.

Look at the map at the front of this guide. Notice where the mountain is. What is at the opposite end of the island? Why is the position of Castle Rock so appropriate?

Order

The island is described as 'roughly boat-shaped'. Interestingly, the boys never seriously consider building a boat to escape – they wait for a boat to come to them. Why might Golding have wanted to keep the boys on the island?

Notice that the boys, whilst looking at the boat-shaped island, 'felt that the boat was moving steadily astern'. The shape of the island is allegorical (used to symbolise a deeper moral meaning). If the boat (island) is sailing, which way is it going? What does this imply about the way the lives of the boys are going? A few paragraphs back Ralph stands on his head. What is the symbolism of this? Golding uses many subtle hints like these and you should be alert for them when reading the book.

Candle buds

Simon

The boys find buds on some bushes. How do their different reactions illustrate the differences in their characters? Notice how Simon says they are 'like candles'. Think about what Simon represents in the novel, and why his naming of the buds is appropriate. (Where would you expect to see candles burning? What do the candles represent?)

21

Jack is not able to kill... not yet

Jack is seen here as still being a product of civilisation. He is unable to kill 'because of the enormity of the knife descending ... the unbearable blood.' Notice the change in Jack after his first successful hunt.

Jack

Chapter 2

A meeting is called. Ralph wants the boys' position to be understood by everyone, and explains the need for law and order. It is established that whoever holds the conch has the right to speak and be listened to. A boy of about six is persuaded to speak by the smaller children. He has a large mulberry-coloured birthmark across one side of his face. He tells the group that he saw a 'beastie' in the woods at night. The younger children seem frightened by this talk. Ralph and the other older boys dismiss the idea of a beast, but Jack spoils the reassuring effect of this by saying that they can make sure when they go hunting. Ralph explains the need to build shelters to sleep in, and a fire to attract possible rescuers.

The boys dash up the mountain to build a signal fire. A vast pile of dead wood is set alight. They use Piggy's glasses to start the fire because they have no matches. The boys agree that special groups will have to be on duty to keep the fire going. Jack volunteers his hunters for this job. Piggy notices that the fire has set the jungle alight. The boys watch in horror as a quarter of a mile square of forest vegetation blazes.

Piggy tries to warn the group about the perils of irresponsible behaviour, but they only make fun of him. When he points out that the little boy with the birthmark has been missing since the fire, there is an atmosphere of discomfort and shame.

"There aren't any grown-ups."

Ralph's natural inclination is towards orderly and democratic assemblies. Notice how the conch is to be used as the visible symbol of authority and to show who has the right to speak. How does Golding convey the idea that Jack's notion of fun includes bullying, punishment and violence? Can you find more evidence of this later in the novel?

The conch

The boys think the island is wonderful: "It's like in a book."

The references to children's books illustrate the adventure and excitement which are offered to children through imaginative fiction. The boys' experience on the island does not parallel stories in these unrealistic books.

It was typical of earlier writers to think in terms of 'British' virtues. These are shown here in the immediate attempt to bring democracy to the island. The difference between Golding and many of the earlier writers is that they present such virtues as being permanent and unchanging; Golding reveals how easily savagery can take over from order. After all, in 'normal' life, none of the boys represented order more than Jack Merridew.

Sugaring the pill?

Golding did not want to make his novel too realistic because 'People do not much like moral lessons. The pill has to be sugared, has to be witty or entertaining, or engaging in some way or another.' Talking about *Lord of the Flies*, he said: 'If the pill is not sufficiently sugared it will not be swallowed. If the moral is terrible enough he [the author] will be regarded as inhuman; and if the edge of his parable cuts deeply enough, he will be crucified.'

Do you think that the novel's moral is terrible and Golding's view of people 'inhuman'? Or do you think that he has managed to 'sugar the pill' enough?

Ralph and Piggy

Ralph

Ralph is in no doubt that grown-ups will rescue them. He thinks the boys can have fun whilst they are waiting. In contrast, Piggy shows that he has a sense of priorities. He is not afraid to speak out, even when what he has to say is unpopular. Ralph tells the assembly that he thinks there are two important things in life on the island – fun and rescue.

The beast appears

Littluns

One of the littluns says that he is afraid of a 'beastie'. The word 'beast' is used in many ways in the novel. On this occasion, what the littlun calls 'a snake thing' is simply an optical illusion created by the creepers. Here, 'the beast' could simply be a small child's nightmare. Can you think of deeper meanings? (Think of what it was that destroyed innocence in the Garden of Eden.)

You cannot write about the collapse of civilisation without taking account of fear: rational argument is not (and has no hope of being) able to remove it. There will later be enough apparently hard evidence to add to the nightmares for the beast to become real to most of the boys.

Fire: protection and destruction

Traditionally fire symbolises power and hope as well as fear and destruction. In Greek legends Prometheus was punished by the Gods for stealing fire from Mount Olympus and giving it to Mankind, thereby empowering Man. Fire brings warmth, comfort and a sense of safety, but equally can destroy everything in its path. You can think about the ways in which Golding uses all the different feelings attached to fire in this novel. A similar sort of ambiguity surrounds the hunters: obtaining food necessary for survival/destroying the community by wanton killing.

Piggy is both wise and vulnerable

Piggy

Piggy hates irresponsible behaviour. Why do you think he criticises the boys for behaving 'like a crowd of kids', when that is exactly what they are? He is helpless and terrified when Jack takes his glasses to make a fire, in case he doesn't return them. Piggy is completely dependent upon his glasses, and therefore on the goodwill of those who borrow them.

Order

Jack denies Piggy the right to speak. In contrast, Ralph supports Piggy's claim to speak because he has the conch. Is Jack showing signs of wishing to be a dictator? Does Ralph believe in democracy?

Does Jack say one thing then do another?

Jack

Carefully read Jack's speech: 'I agree… do the right things.' Compare his beliefs here with his behaviour later in the novel. Does Jack's character worsen as the novel progresses? Was he in fact all that noble to begin with?

The use of animal imagery

At first the flame of the fire is 'a squirrel', leaping from tree to tree, but as the fire grows, so the image becomes a fiercer animal that 'gnaws'. Then the image becomes a jaguar, a predator which 'creeps on its belly' towards its prey. Can you see how Golding draws a parallel with the destructive passion developing amongst the boys?

Notice how the language hints at future events: Piggy glances 'into hell' and later, 'the crowd' (not 'the boys') stand 'silent as death'.

Piggy reprimands the other boys about the fire

Jack

Piggy

With what words does Ralph respond to Piggy's accusations of carelessness? Notice how Jack repeats the words a short while later. How does Jack react to accurate, reasonable criticism? What do you learn about Jack from this? Do you agree that Piggy's weakness is that although there is often good sense in what he says, he seems unable to convince the group of anything? Ralph is the only one who listens to Piggy's ideas. Which other character does nobody listen to?

Piggy represents the power of 'conscience'. He frequently cautions the others to consider what grown-ups would think of their behaviour. Why is it not surprising that Piggy is the one to notice that a littlun is missing? Why do you think Piggy is so 'adult' for his age? (Consider his upbringing, and how his isolation from 'normal' boyish behaviour because of his physique and ill-health might have affected his character.)

What do you think of Piggy from the first couple of chapters? Would life have been different on the island if Piggy had been voted chief? Compare your attitude to Piggy now with what you think of him by the end of the novel. Notice how Ralph's attitude towards Piggy has changed by the end of the book. Try to pinpoint exactly when Ralph changes his mind about Piggy. (Look towards the end of Chapter 4.)

'The crowd was as silent as death'

The first death is of the littlun with the birthmark. Later, Simon and Piggy die, and they too have physical 'defects'. Do any of the other boys have physical defects like these three? Is it true that only the boys with physical defects get killed? Why does Golding make this happen? Were the three boys vulnerable simply because they were not physically perfect? Or is this Golding's way of hinting that these characters are special, and that we are to think more deeply about exactly what makes them outsiders?

Darkness and death

The first death is important in discussing what went wrong on the island. Who is responsible for it? 'Half the boys' get to their feet at the mention of fire, Jack, 'among them', calls on the boys to follow him. Jack plays a part, certainly, but it would be wrong to blame him totally for the hysteria: this first loss of innocence involves the boys as a group.

'A tree exploded in the fire...'

The Bible story of the Garden of Eden presents the snake as evil. Snake images are used in this way throughout the novel. The burning creepers look like snakes and as such are something to fear. The last sentence of this chapter contains powerful symbolism. Traditionally, when might you hear a drum roll? Is this side of the island really 'unfriendly'? The description at the beginning of Chapter 7 explains why the boys might feel this way.

Chapter 3

Jack is learning to hunt. Others should have been building huts but they have grown apathetic and prefer to swim or laze around. Ralph complains that the boys prefer playing to working for the communal good. Two opposing ways of life are already developing on the island. Jack hunts and kills whilst Ralph makes efforts to get the boys shelter and rescue. The fears of the littluns are discussed but the boys are unable to put their feelings into words.

Simon wanders off into the jungle on his own. On his way through the acres of fruit trees, he helps some littluns reach the ripe fruit. He finds a hideaway in thick jungle foliage and here he sits and thinks about the many beauties of the living things around him.

'The silence of the forest...'

Whilst practising hunting techniques, Jack is startled by 'a harsh cry that seemed to come out of the abyss of ages.' This underlines the gap that exists between modern civilisation and past ages, when primitive man had to hunt in order to survive.

When he returns, Jack tries to talk about the primitive feeling for the hunt which is growing inside him. Outwardly, there is 'madness' in his eyes. List the words and phrases which describe Jack's body movements changing from those of a civilised boy into those of a hunter.

Savagery

"They're batty."

Jack's growth into the leading savage contrasts with the other boys' attempts to maintain a civilised society on the beach. Ralph gives two reasons for building huts. What are they? The collapse of a hut means a heavier workload for Ralph, but what does it represent in terms of civilisation on the island? Why are the boys so reluctant to build huts?

Order

The collapse of civilisation on the island (the 'going wrong' mentioned in Essay 2, page 62) proceeds by negatives as well as positives. It is not only the beast within (exemplified by the tribe) that destroys it, but equally the inability to cope with such things as providing shelter.

Jack, Ralph and Simon have been discussing the littluns' nightmares and their intense fear at night. Jack admits to sensing something fearful when he is alone in the jungle. To what does he compare this feeling? What is Golding telling us here about the dark side of the human mind? (Re-read the section 'The beast' on pages 13–14 for help with these questions.)

Ralph and Jack 'faced each other on the bright beach'

Manual work has no appeal for Piggy. He does not help Ralph build the huts. Can you connect this with Piggy's belief that 'life is scientific'? Notice the widening gap between Jack and Ralph.

Piggy

Simon

Simon's bright eyes suggest to Ralph that he both is 'delightfully gay' (meaning

Simon

happy and carefree) and 'wicked'. What do you think the brightness of Simon's eyes illustrates? Events and images surrounding Simon often parallel Bible stories of Christ. Simon helps his fellow humans, struggles with 'the devil', and is finally killed by people who fail to understand him. Golding uses pearl and opal as colour images in connection with Simon. Why do you think he chooses these luminous colours?

Read the description of the acres of fruit trees. Golding describes the world

Nature

of nature as the Garden of Eden. Given this religious reference, what is Golding suggesting in the rest of this chapter?

Read the description of Simon finding his den in the foliage. The butterfly motif recurs the next time Simon visits his den. What do you think the butterflies symbolise? Think about their delicacy and their fragile, short-lived beauty.

Golding's beautiful description of the foliage as night falls serves to portray Simon at one with the natural world. Why is this appropriate? Both Jack and Simon go into the jungle alone – but Jack is pleased when other boys join him, whereas Simon wants to make sure that nobody follows him.

Chapter 4

Life on the island takes on its own rhythm. By noon, the unbearable heat and light create mirages. Piggy explains these in a typically rational way. The dark hours create a restless fearfulness amongst the boys. The littluns pass the days in aimless play, and seem to have forgotten their true situation. Some older boys, notably Roger, begin to treat them unkindly by throwing stones and spoiling their innocent pastimes.

Jack uses clay to paint his face in order to camouflage himself while hunting. The sight of his reflection is a subconscious turning-point for him, for the mask releases him from normal civilised behaviour. Later, Ralph, Piggy and Simon are talking when they see the smoke from a steamship on the horizon. But the signal fire on the mountain has gone out and the ship passes. All the hunters return jubilant with pig meat, and there is a confrontation between the two groups about the fire being out. Jack hits Piggy and breaks his glasses, then apologises – but with bad grace. The pig is roasted over the relit fire. The boys act out the scene of the kill. The ritual is to become part of their way of life. Ralph decides to call an assembly, even though it is late.

Strange things happened at midday

The lagoon is both a symbol of safety and a place of illusions. Notice how

Nature

this contrasts with the sea on the other side of the island. What effect does the simile 'the sun gazed down like an angry eye' have? The intense midday light creates optical illusions. How do the boys react to these illusions? Piggy's approach is typically scientific.

Note how civilised time – represented by watches – has been replaced by nature's time, and nature's 'rhythms'. Piggy wants to build a sundial. Read on in this chapter and try to discover why he should want to do this.

Percival

Percival is a pathetic character. What does he represent in terms of what the

Littluns

children have lost? Golding describes the 'corporate life' of the littluns. Their 'generic title' (a group name rather than personal names) reinforces our sense of their dwindling individuality. Younger than the others, they have had less time to learn the ways of society. They seem to be losing the refinements of civilisation. Do you consider the older boys neglectful of the littluns? Is it their fault that the littluns suffer from eating too much unripe fruit?

'They had built castles...'

Littluns

Sand castles are being built by the littluns – symbolic of a child's sense of romance and adventure. This description neatly conjures up the atmosphere of very small children at play. What changes do the sunshine and daylight bring? How would you describe the way the littluns feel? Are they really happy?

Roger and Maurice come out of the forest

Roger

How does Roger reveal some indication of his hidden, sadistic tendencies? Do you find Roger's actions surprising? Golding wrote: 'I have lived for many years with small boys, and understand and know them with awful precision.' Looking at Roger as one example, do you think that Golding is right?

You might find it interesting to see how many references to Roger you can find before his final emergence as a figure of terror. Mainly he is an unobtrusive character, his personality hidden, hinted at in incidents like this. Is he the most changed character on the island (as in Essay 3, page 64)?

Henry plays with the creatures at the water's edge

Littluns

What is Golding indicating in his description of Henry controlling the creatures at the sea's edge? Notice Henry's absorption in play and how he treats the little animals. Look at the way Roger behaves towards Henry. Roger's behaviour is only tempered by his upbringing in the civilised world. What is Golding saying about the character of humankind?

The mask appears

Jack

Savagery

Jack brings coloured clay to paint his face. What reason does he have for doing this? Do you think that at this point Jack understands the power of a mask?

How does the mask widen the gap between Ralph and Jack? Ask yourself what Jack is becoming and to what Ralph is clinging. A painted mask offers an external picture of what is happening within Jack – he is regressing to a primitive form. Jack sees his reflection as an 'awesome stranger'. Why do you think he is so delighted with this? From what does the mask release him?

Notice how personal appearance is important to Jack in his lust for power. Contrast this with Ralph's worries about his increasingly dirty and savage appearance.

'Piggy wore the remainders of a pair of shorts'

Can you extract from this passage a further example of what makes Piggy so

Piggy

different from the others? He is described as 'an outsider, not only by accent'. Piggy comes from a lower-middle class/working class background. His father is dead and his mother's whereabouts unknown. This contrasts with Ralph's comfortable home life and the choir's public-school upbringing. How are the contrasts between Piggy and the others displayed in the language they use?

Piggy has many problems including the class divide between him and the others (see Essay 3, page 64). Even when expressing thoughts of great importance he is hampered by poor grammar: 'I can't see no smoke'. He is the constant outsider, even the only one whose hair does not grow!

The ship appears

When Ralph saw a ship sail by that might have rescued them, 'he reached inside himself for the worst word he knew'. What does the particular word

Ralph

he uses tell you about his background? Piggy and Ralph show their strong love of civilisation as Jack moves further towards savagery.

The hunters return

After the first hunt, Jack proudly tells the others that he cut the pig's throat, and yet he 'twitched as he said it.' What does this indicate about him? What effect might the hunters' chanting have upon them? (Think of a football crowd.)

At this moment, Jack and Ralph are worlds apart in both experience and emotion. Jack is jubilant after his first hunting success. Ralph is in bitter despair at the lost chance of rescue. How important is rescue to Jack now?

Piggy's glasses are broken

Throughout the book, Piggy shows that clear sight comes not only from the

Piggy

eyes but also from the mind. Piggy sees the boys' situation clearly. His glasses are a symbol of understanding and reason.

The success of the hunt has released Jack from the civilised need to keep back his aggressive tendencies, and he strikes Piggy, breaking his glasses. Both Piggy and Ralph accused him of being irresponsible, so why does Jack hit only Piggy? The breaking of one lens of the glasses symbolises the beginning of the loss of reasonable behaviour on the island.

Jack can be described as an atavist. This is someone who reverts to the behaviour and attitudes of their distant ancestors. Jack redirects his aggression from the pig to Piggy, smashing one of his lenses.

Golding wrote that the civilisation on the island 'breaks down in blood and terror because the boys are suffering from the terrible disease of being human.' As you read the novel, notice how the disease takes hold and grows worse.

"You didn't hunt."

Simon

In the face of Jack's cruel refusal to give Piggy any meat, Simon shares his. Simon's action here is kind and civilised so why does he 'lower his face in shame'? What is the significance of Ralph standing with his hands full of meat 'among the ashes of the signal fire'?

"Where did you find the pig?"

As Jack and the hunters describe their first kill, they use words which show they are revelling in the knowledge that they deliberately spilled the pig's blood. Notice that the excuse for killing – that the boys need meat – is not the real reason for it. Jack likes killing for its own sake because it gives him a sense of power. Remember that earlier, Jack was so excited about the slaughter of the pig that he felt no guilt for letting the signal fire go out.

Savagery   Jack and his group take up a ritual chant: 'Kill the pig. Cut her throat. Bash her in.' Why do you think Ralph now decides to call a meeting, 'even if we have to go on into the dark'? Think about why this might be one of his greatest mistakes.

Notice that Jack's rage is described as 'elemental and awe-inspiring'. In the silence that follows he 'looked round for understanding but found only respect'. Understanding and reason are being replaced by more 'elemental' forces on the island.

■ Self-test questions Chapters 1–4

Uncover the plot

Delete two of the three alternatives given, to find the correct plot. Beware possible misconceptions and muddles.

While evacuating children from a war zone, a plane/a parachutist/an atom bomb crashes on a remote tropical island. Two young boys, Ralph and Piggy, meet up and Ralph blows a megaphone/trumpet/conch shell to frighten wild animals/gather up the rest of the survivors/attract rescuers. The group of boys elect Piggy/Ralph/Jack as their leader; this annoys Jack, the shy/confident/blond leader of the choir, but he is appeased when Ralph volunteers the choir as the army/fire tenders/hunters. Ralph, Jack and Simon explore the island and find it uninhabited/get lost/kill a pig. Another meeting is called, at which it is decided that the conch should give the person holding/blowing/smashing it the right to speak; some of the smaller ones describe their fear of a 'beastie' that comes out of the jungle at night. The group starts a signal fire using a bow and arrow/Piggy's glasses/matches, which rages out of control and kills one of the littluns. Simon/Piggy/Jack learns to hunt pigs/snakes/beasts, while Ralph struggles to get the other boys to help build shelters. Jack paints his face and takes the choir, who are supposed to be tending the fire, on a hunt. The fire goes out/will not light/burns up the forest and a storm/ship/plane passes in the distance. There is a tense confrontation when the hunters return, during which Jack attacks Ralph/Piggy/Simon and breaks his glasses. Matters are partially resolved as they roast and eat the pig, and Ralph calls another meeting.

Who? What? Why? Where? When? How?

1   What realisation causes Ralph glee and Piggy concern when they first assess their situation? What is Jack's reaction to the same realisation?
2   What does Piggy hope the boys will not do?
3   Why do the boys choose Ralph as their leader?
4   How do Jack, Ralph and Simon react to their encounter with the piglet?
5   What compulsion begins to 'swallow Jack up'?
6   Where does Simon go to on his own?
7   How do the smaller boys spend their days?

8　What stops Roger from hitting Henry with the stones?

9　Why do you think Bill 'falls silent and blunders away through the bushes' when Jack paints his face?

10　Who gives meat to Piggy, and why does he then 'lower his face in shame'?

Who is this?

1　Who 'might make a boxer, as far as width and heaviness of shoulders went, but there was a mildness about his mouth and eyes that proclaimed no devil'?

2　Who 'moved among the crowd, asking names and frowning to remember them'?

3　Who has 'two light blue eyes, frustrated now, and turning, or ready to turn, to anger'?

4　According to whom, who is 'always throwing a faint'?

5　Who is 'a slight, furtive boy whom no one knew, who kept to himself with an inner intensity of avoidance and secrecy'?

6　Who has 'The opaque, mad look' in his eyes?

7　Who is 'a small, skinny boy, his chin pointed, and his eyes so bright they had deceived Ralph into thinking him delightfully gay and wicked'?

8　Who 'was an outsider, not only by accent, which did not matter…'?

Creative colour

Golding's use of colour is precise, detailed and significant. Comment on the effect(s) of the following colours. (Think about how they might emphasise themes, particular aspects of character, or work as symbols.)

1　'In colour the shell was deep cream, touched here and there with fading pink.' (Chapter 1)

2　'To put on a grey shirt once more was strangely pleasing.' (Chapter 1)

3　'Inside the floating cloak he was tall, thin and bony: and his hair was red beneath the black cap.' (Chapter 1)

4　'(His eyes) were bright blue, eyes that in this frustration seemed bolting and nearly mad.' (Chapter 3)

5　'The candle buds stirred. Their green sepals drew back a little and the white tips of flowers rose delicately to meet the open air.' (Chapter 3)

Follow my leader

Both Jack and Ralph are 'leaders', but in very different ways. With this in mind, answer the following questions.

1　What qualities does Jack reveal in his treatment of the choir when he first arrives on the beach?

2　What does Jack want to be called, and why?

3　Why does Jack say he ought to be chief? When he is not elected, how does Ralph react?

4　What does Piggy's alliance with Ralph reveal about Piggy himself? How does he feel about Jack?

5　When the fire goes out and Jack and Ralph confront each other, how does Ralph assert his leadership?

Chapter 5

Ralph realises the importance of making the boys develop a sense of responsibility towards the common good. At the assembly he criticises them severely. Many littluns are terrified at night, and Ralph, helped by Piggy, tries to allay their fears. But Jack plays on their terror and Ralph's near-success is ruined. Talk of beasts and monsters spreads through the group. Simon tries to explain that there is no real beast, that evil comes from within people, but the boys fail to understand him.

The assembly falls from disorder into outright chaos. They have a vote about whether there may be ghosts, and overwhelmingly the boys vote 'yes'. Ralph cannot regain control. Jack says that he will not obey the rules, and the meeting breaks up. Many of the boys begin to dance and chant in a circle on the beach. Ralph considers resigning from the leadership but Piggy and Simon persuade him not to. Piggy admits to being scared of Jack. The split between the two groups is evident.

'Again he fell into that strange mood...'

Ralph

Ralph is the character in the novel who learns the most. Here he asks himself some difficult questions about appearance, perception and reality, even though 'speculation was so foreign to him'. At times Ralph finds he is no longer sure of his own standards. Sometimes he cannot think straight. Does Ralph's clarity of thought improve as the novel progresses?

Ralph has come to respect Piggy

Piggy

Ralph recognises Piggy's value as a thinker. Which words show that Ralph now understands it is a mistake to judge people and things by their appearances? Ralph finds himself thinking more deeply than he is accustomed to. What conclusion does he come to at this stage about Piggy?

The assembly begins

As the boys take their places for the assembly, notice which group chooses to

Order

sit on Ralph's right and who sits to his left. Can you see the significance here? Think about the terms 'left' and 'right' as used in twentieth-century politics.

Ralph lectures the boys on their insanitary habits – they are soiling their own living areas. What does this indicate about the state of their civilisation? Ralph says that they ought to die before they let the fire go out: 'the fire is the most important thing'. From your reading of the novel up to this point, what do you think are the reasons for the boys' apathy?

'There was a row immediately.'

Ralph is still closely connected to the adult world of order and stability. Do

Roger

you think that this is why he has a struggle to understand why things change? Do you think that Jack's increasing power over the others is helped by a flaw in Ralph's leadership? If so, what is it? If you think Ralph has no flaws in the way he leads the boys, what is it that goes wrong? Does he make a mistake?

In many essays (including all three in the back of this guide) it helps to consider how far Ralph is responsible for the collapse of civilisation. It is difficult to criticise him: he tries with earnest fairness to make the best of the situation and we usually share his viewpoint, but think about how he handles, for example, Jack or the fear within the group.

'Jack stood up and took the conch.'

The beast

Ralph tries to erase the littluns' fears by talking sensibly, but Jack ruins this. Jack tells the littluns that fear is within them all and they must learn to live with it. Jack seems to want to make the others believe in the beast. How could this be of help to him?

"I got the conch!"

Piggy has a typically rational argument against being afraid. Can you say why

Piggy

he feels this way? After all, he is particularly physically vulnerable. You might have expected him to be the most afraid. But Piggy is trying to remove the boys' fear whilst Jack is trying to reinforce it. What does this reveal about their different characters?

Piggy believes that science has the answer to fear and superstition. This illustrates Piggy's 'adult' clear-sightedness and his civilised way of thinking. Notice the irony of Piggy's use of the 'double negative'. This is the difference between what he says and what he means. He says 'I know there isn't no beast…but I know there isn't no fear either'; but 'is *not no* beast' and 'is *not no* fear' actually mean that there *is* a beast and there *is* fear. When Piggy and, later, Simon suggest that the thing to fear is lodged within themselves, they are voicing one of the fundamental themes of the novel.

Both Piggy and Simon are deliberately murdered in the end. What point of view, what opinion, do Piggy and Simon alone share unwaveringly throughout the novel? (Golding said about *Lord of the Flies* that it taught the lesson that 'the only enemy of man is inside him.')

'A whiteness in the gloom…'

Simon

Simon, although self-conscious, feels 'a perilous necessity to speak'. He tries to explain his feeling that the beast may be inside them. 'Humankind's essential illness' is the evil force within man. Simon is struggling to find a way to explain this. He is ridiculed by Jack and his group. What does this suggest about the way society treats the mystic or prophet?

Was this assembly a mistake?

Order

Much of Chapter 5 is concerned with discussing fear and the beast. Notice that fear makes the boys more irrational as darkness falls. Do you agree with Ralph that he 'was wrong to call this assembly so late'?

Ralph's failure to keep order is partly his fault and partly the fault of others. Which mistakes does Ralph know he has made? Are there any he is not aware of? Why does Ralph become unpopular?

Look at Piggy's speech, where he separates himself from the boys' irrational behaviour and beliefs: 'I didn't vote for no ghosts!' Jack's response shows his total disregard for Piggy.

"Bollocks to the rules!"

The assembly and the conch are dismissed in this one phrase. Jack challenges

Jack

Ralph's suitability for the leadership. Ralph responds by telling Jack he is 'breaking the rules'. This is a point of crisis in the novel. Does Ralph's faith in democratic behaviour now strike you as ridiculous? Think about when the novel was written.

Jack's shout: 'Bollocks to the rules!' brings into the open his changing character and intentions. Re-read what he thought about rules in Chapter 1. How has he changed? What is he challenging now?

Lord of the Flies, as a well-planned novel, is full of significant turning points: 'the first sign of cruelty', etc. Constant gradual change is Golding's method. However, the moment when Jack shouts 'Bollocks to the rules!' has to be a key moment, denying the basis for their whole life-style.

Bear in mind that Golding was concerned about the way many people were thinking after the Second World War had ended. He wrote: 'You think that now the war is over and an evil thing destroyed, you are safe because you are naturally kind and decent. But I know why the thing rose in Germany. I know it could happen in any country. It could happen here.'

"He hates me. I dunno why."

Order

Piggy speaks of *his* fear – fear of people. He recognises that the bully in Jack could lead to danger for himself. Why is it that Piggy understands more about the way people behave than Ralph does?

Ralph's wish about grown-ups: 'If only they could get a message to us' and his desire for a 'sign or something' acknowledges the need for adult authority.

Chapter 6

In the night a pilot drops by parachute from an air battle many miles above the island. The dead body is carried by the wind to the mountain top where it is jammed between the rocks. Next morning, when Samneric go to relight the fire, they see the shape of the parachutist and then rush in terror to the others, saying that they have seen the beast. Ralph and Jack lead a search party for the beast, leaving Piggy to take care of the littluns.

'Yard by yard, puff by puff...'

The dead parachutist is the 'sign' for which Ralph asked in the last chapter, but is not, perhaps, the one he would have preferred. The fact that the adult is dead gives us a hint about the condition of the world away from the island.

Ralph is often associated with yellow – the colour of the sun. Can you think why this might be appropriate? (Think about why it is appropriate that Jack is often associated with red and black.)

Jack openly refuses to recognise the authority of the conch.

The beast   Which phrase suggests that he considers the actions of the hunters to be outside the control of the assembly?

Simon sees 'the beast' as human

With the arrival of the parachutist, the idea of a beast has been given a physical form. But on the hunt to find it, Simon feels 'a flicker of incredulity'. There follows a good example of his intuitive intelligence, his 'inward sight'. Why do you think Simon's 'picture of a human' is described as being both 'heroic

Simon   and sick'?

If Roger is not the most changed character (Essay 3, page 64), maybe Simon is. The novel is partly based on contrasts between material worlds (school/isolation, civilisation/tribalism) and practical priorities (fire and shelter/hunting and food) and it is Simon who gives it a visionary dimension.

Castle Rock

Castle Rock eventually becomes a fortress for Jack's tribe. Why is this place

a suitable setting for savagery and superstition? What does Ralph think of it?

Notice how Golding uses personification to describe the sea; that is, he describes it as a living thing; 'the swell... seemed like the breathing of some stupendous creature'. Compare this

Nature   with the description near the start of Chapter 4 when Golding describes 'the other side' of the island.

'A sound behind him made him turn'

Jack joins Ralph on the hunt for the beast. Why are these moments of conversation between the two boys so touching, so poignant? What breaks it up? Which event towards the end of the chapter hints at things to come?

Chapter 7

Ralph daydreams as the search for the beast continues. Simon is intuitively optimistic that Ralph will get home safely, but Ralph says that Simon is 'batty'. A pig charges out of the undergrowth and Ralph has a taste of the thrill of hunting. He joins in the chanting and ritual mime. A boy is almost killed during this play-acting. Jack sees something on the mountain top and Ralph and Roger climb up with him to investigate. By now it is growing dark. In their fear they interpret the shape of the dead parachutist as a 'great ape' and they race away from it in terror.

'A little fall of the heart'

Ralph

Notice Ralph's concern about his filthy condition. A little further on he experiences 'a little fall of the heart'. This phrase suggests that he has begun to mind his dirty and unkempt appearance. Ralph's behaviour is deteriorating – he bites his nails, he daydreams, he becomes forgetful. Why do you think this is?

The unfriendly side of the island

Notice the contrast of the 'other side of the island' to their own side. The

Nature

opposite side of the island is 'utterly different' because the cold sea hardens the images. There are no 'mirages' here, instead the horizon is a 'hard, clipped blue'. On their side the lagoon protects them and 'one might dream of rescue'. Why does the lagoon side encourage daydreams?

Notice the language used by Golding to describe the sea on this side of the island. What is the effect of words like 'suck', 'sink', 'plaster down', 'rise', 'roar' and 'irresistibly'? The two sides of the island are rather like the two 'sides' of human beings – the good and the evil. The action has moved away from the 'friendly side' of both.

'Simon was speaking almost in his ear.'

Simon

How far do you consider Simon's words to Ralph to be prophetic? When Ralph calls Simon 'batty', what does this tell us about his understanding of Simon? If Ralph does not value what Simon says, will anyone else?

Notice that Simon speaks very softly to Ralph, 'almost in his ear' – like an inner voice, or perhaps the voice of conscience? Contrast this with the way Jack speaks.

Ralph's daydream of home

Ralph

Ralph's dreams of his old home cannot help him cope with his present situation. The images of books suggest a child's ideas of travel, adventure and fear. But this is the view from the comfort of a normal, civilised life. How different is Ralph now from when he used to read these books? Why do you think Ralph needs to remind himself of his old life?

Hunting, wounding, hurting

Savagery

The 'play' hunt with Robert as the boar has a noticeable effect on Ralph. Think carefully about the sentence, 'the desire to squeeze and hurt was overmastering.' What is Golding suggesting here? Notice again the chant and its effect.

In assessing the role of Ralph (as in Essay 1, page 61) it is important to note that he shares many of Jack's enthusiasms, but is driven by a sense of duty. You can find a bond of adventure between the two early in the novel. Even here Ralph is 'carried away by a sudden thick excitement' which then makes him uneasy.

Berengaria was the wife of Richard the Lionheart. She is credited with saving her husband's life by sucking a wound made by a poisoned arrow. Is there an ominous ring to Simon's comment about Berengaria? Think about the symbolism which surrounds Simon and the word 'wound'. Now think about how Jack and the idea of wounding are related in the novel.

Who is pretending?

In his own mind, Ralph tries to keep what is happening on the same level as

Ralph

play, like a rugby game. Rugby is a game that in a secure world is played strictly to the rules. Play on the island develops into something different. What do you think makes Ralph say, 'Just a game'? Why does he say this 'uneasily'?

Jack and his hunters plan a mock hunt – a ritual performance. How can you tell that the evil, sadistic elements within them are coming out? Look carefully at what is said, especially about using a littlun.

Simon goes back alone through the jungle

Simon

Simon offers to go back alone through the dark jungle. This is important. If he had stayed and seen the beast with the others he might have established the truth. Look at how Jack talks 'in a queer tight voice' about not letting anything happen to

Piggy. Ralph feels Jack's 'antagonism'. The tension between the two boys builds up during the trek.

"I'm going up the mountain to look for the beast... coming?"

Notice all the references to darkness during this trip. Ralph has learned by experience not to undertake things in the dark. (When?) Notice how Jack tests Ralph. Roger, whom we already know to be destructive, is one of those present on the climb to find the 'beast'. Simon is no longer there. What does this tell us about the shifting of power from Ralph to Jack and his hunters?

Although Ralph's leadership is disintegrating, he does not lack courage – but everybody flees from the 'beast'. Golding's description of the decomposing parachutist skilfully merges the two concepts of beast and human; 'Something like a great ape' he calls it, with 'the ruin of a face'. Notice this subtle echo of the masks worn by the hunters.

The beast

Chapter 8

Inevitably, reports of what the boys have seen on the mountain top become distorted. Jack and Ralph are in open rivalry for the leadership. Finally, after he has lost a challenge for the leadership because no one will vote Ralph out of being chief, the humiliated Jack leaves the assembly, refusing 'to play' anymore. Simon speaks to the group but without effect. Piggy suggests building a new signal fire near the platform. They then notice that many boys have gone off, presumably to join Jack's group. Simon goes off alone to his favourite hiding place in the forest.

Jack organises his followers. They hunt and kill a pig as a sacrifice to the beast. Simon witnesses this event from his hiding place. As Ralph and Piggy discuss the break-up of their society, they are attacked by Jack's band of savages, who steal burning sticks from the fire. Jack announces he is chief of a new tribe and invites everyone to a feast that night. The heat, humidity and Simon's physical condition cause him to hallucinate as he stares at the fly-covered pig's head. He has a 'conversation' with the head, the Lord of the Flies. The head warns Simon of the impossibility of escape from the beast. It says the evil is within the boys themselves. The Lord of the Flies threatens Simon, who faints.

The beast is real

Ralph is now convinced of the reality of the beast. What is the effect of the

symbolism and coincidence in Ralph's comment, 'And now that thing squats by the fire as though it didn't want us to be rescued–'? Would the effect have been different if the parachutist had landed on the beach, or in the scar, or on top of Castle Rock? It is important that the 'beast' appears on the

The beast

mountain top. Why?

"I've called an assembly"

The conch

Jack takes the initiative in formally calling an assembly. Is this the only time he uses the conch? Look at the words Golding uses to describe the way Jack holds the conch. Does Jack hold it like this out of respect for the authority it represents? What are his motives in calling this meeting? Carefully study the way Jack uses the democratic procedure of the assembly to try to manipulate the group. On which of their emotions is he playing?

The challenge to Ralph's leadership

Ralph

Why do you think the group would not vote against Ralph as leader? Does it say something about their fear of speaking out? Of whom might they be afraid?

Ralph, who seems quite a good person, does not make a particularly good leader. What makes a good leader? Think about what might have happened if Jack had been elected leader from the start: would things have turned out better, or worse? Ralph tries to keep order by using rules. But people do not always keep to the rules. How do you imagine Jack and his choir would have kept order?

"I'm not going to play any longer."

Jack

Consider the irony of Jack's words. Play has been transformed from something harmless into a hysterical ritual. Yet there is pathos here too: can you identify exactly why Jack's comment is so touching?

"I think we ought to climb the mountain."

Simon

How does Simon display self-sacrifice here? Even Piggy cannot understand the point Simon is making. Only Simon is able to recognise that this is the turning-point in their lives on the island. Notice the way the group do not respect or recognise Simon's value.

Piggy suggests making the fire down on the beach

Piggy

How has the assembly's opinion of Piggy changed now that Jack has left? Contrast Piggy's intellect with that of Simon. Piggy is intensely practical. How would you describe the way Simon thinks? Compare the way the littluns dance and sing here and the way Jack's tribe do it later.

Piggy has assisted with the building of the new fire. He even lights the fire himself. This is important, because it shows that Piggy is no longer an outsider. Why is this?

Ralph says they must have a list of names

Some of the other boys have left the group, presumably to join Jack. Piggy's humour is ironic: 'I expect they won't play either.' Which boys are the first to go? Can you see why? The boys prepare a 'feast' for Ralph. Compare this feast with Jack's in Chapter 9.

Simon again enters the jungle alone

Simon retreats to his private den. Notice his mood of self-denial. Compare Simon at this point with Christ in the wilderness. What did they both have ahead of them? In his private place, Simon is surrounded by nature. Notice the butterfly – a symbol of delicate perfection in air. Look at which form of insect life displays itself to Simon the next time we see him in his den.

Simon

The choir has undergone a change

Not long ago, 'their voices had been the song of angels'. What have the choir now become? What do you think is the significance of the black caps they retain? (Think of what British judges sometimes used to wear on their heads, and when.) Jack tells the group, 'I'm going to be chief'. What does this indicate about the political organisation of Jack's tribe?

Savagery

It is important to see that Golding here is making clear that the spirit and discipline of the choir have not been destroyed, just transformed. What we now see is a debased version of the choir we saw first and once more they are taking part in religious ritual, equally debased, to appease the beast.

Jack is now chief

Jack's surname is Merridew. The name means 'lord of the place'. It is

significant that this is the name Jack first wanted to be called by. It is not difficult to think of Jack as the villain of the novel, but is this altogether fair? Was Jack to blame for the death of the littlun with the birthmark? Is it only Jack who is responsible for Simon's death? Who is to blame for Piggy's

Jack   death? Try to decide whether Jack actually knows when he is doing wrong, or whether he is just unable to resist 'the beast' for as long as the others.

"Forget the beast!"

The hunters are in passionate agreement with Jack's proposals. How does he

Savagery

release them from 'the depths of their tormented private lives'? Jack proposes a primitive and superstitious way of appeasing the beast. This marks a further stage in his degeneration. Jack finds that rituals are important to him. For example, how do you think he feels during the episodes of chanting and dancing?

'The pigs lay, bloated bags of fat...'

Pink is an important colour image; it often makes an ironic contrast with the action. Here the 'pink' of the pigs suggests a baby, a vulnerable thing. Look also at the use of pink to describe the island and the conch in Chapter 1. Read carefully the description of the attack and the killing of the sow. Would a real hunter kill a sow with young?

Savagery

Golding's description of the sow's killing is electrified with forceful emotion: 'wedded to her in lust', 'fulfilled upon her'. Why do you think he uses sexual terminology?

The hunt of the sow can be seen as the point when the boys' finally break with their past moral values and innocence. Why is hope for civilised life on the island lost from this moment? The force of destruction, represented by Jack, triumphs over the controls of civilisation, represented by Ralph. Would you agree that the killing of the sow is the climax of the book? Is the real end of the book a climax or an anticlimax?

Violence and 'civilisation'

The violence of war, or the hunt, makes the act of killing thrilling. It releases the hidden, evil side from humankind's inner being. Golding thought evil much more common than many people like to believe. In a 1963 interview he said: 'some have said that the brutality of the novel is impossible. It's not. Look at any newspaper... .' Do you agree with him?

'Here, struck down by the heat...'

Roger

The name Roger means 'famous with the spear'. Notice Golding's interpretation of this in Roger's actions. Think about Roger's part in killing the sow. What evidence can you find that Roger is particularly sadistic?

Jack flicks the dead sow's blood at the others

Savagery

In a primitive celebration of killing, Jack rubs blood over Maurice's face. This is a further example of Jack's commitment to the savage life. By killing the sow, Jack and his band have symbolically killed a mother/parent figure. From this moment on, they are savage and brutal. Their innocence is lost. Think about which characters are absent from the hunt. Do they keep their innocence? The hunters relish their release from civilised behaviour, illustrated here by their language. They are now free to say words like 'ass'.

Roger calls Jack 'Chief' for the first time. Does the tribe ever again refer to him as Jack? The pig's head is stuck on a prepared stake and left as a gift for the beast. Roger later sharpens another stick: how similar is its intended use?

The use of language in the transformation of the boys on the island is interesting. Jack becomes 'chief', no longer an ordinary person (perhaps not even an individual), but remember that he has always been different ('Why should I be Jack? I'm Merridew.') and note the echo of the boys' other life obeying the nameless superior ('sir').

The Lord of the Flies

Simon

The strange conversation Simon has with the Lord of the Flies can be interpreted as a symbolic experience; a conflict between good and evil. Is Simon's conversation with evil real or imagined? Do not worry if you cannot decide. Golding wants you to consider the conversation from all angles, so you should try to find a variety of interpretations.

Simon has turned this part of the jungle into a symbolic church. The beast is on the mountain, and the hunters bring before Simon (without knowing that he is there) what Golding has called 'their false god'. But the false god of the hunters knows Simon is there. A pulse begins to beat in Simon's head. What suggestion is there in the text that Simon may be having an epileptic fit during his conversation with the Lord of the Flies?

Darkness
and death

The pig's head rules the flies just as the evil inside the boys controls their actions. Notice the simile 'tics that buzzed like a saw'. How does this create a contrast with Simon's experience (or hallucination) with the Lord of the Flies? What does Golding mean when he says that Simon's gaze 'was held by that ancient, inescapable recognition'?

Flies feed upon the sow's head, just as the boys have begun to feed on the pigs of the island. What else do the boys almost begin to feed on at the end of the novel?

'Lord of the Flies'

Golding's frequent use of parallels and echoes throughout the novel sometimes includes references to other stories, myths or legends. The name 'Lord of the Flies' is given to the pig's head on a stick by Golding, not by the boys. The name is a literal translation of Beelzebub, the name of the devil in the Bible.

' "You are a silly little boy", said the Lord of the Flies'

Simon's intuitive understanding of the nature of being human enables him to

Simon

envisage a world which is full of wonder and at the same time full of dangers. This is why he can still like Jack. This is why the evil represented as the Lord of the Flies must try to beat Simon. The Lord of the Flies knows Simon's inner feelings. In what way is he trying to win the battle with Simon when he says, 'You like Ralph a lot, don't you? And Piggy, and Jack?'

The beast

In the confrontation between the Lord of the Flies and Simon, notice the parallel with the Bible story of Christ being tempted in the wilderness. Does this help you with yet another interpretation of Simon's 'liking' Jack? The Lord of the Flies tries to persuade Simon that evil in humans is so strong that resistance is useless. Does Simon accept this?

'The laughter shivered again'

Why do you think Golding makes the Lord of the Flies speak 'in the voice

Darkness and death

of a schoolmaster'? Are Simon's 'times' a reference to fits, or to moments of sudden understanding, as in a vision? Perhaps they are both. By the end of Simon's dialogue with the Lord of the Flies, in how many ways can you interpret the 'blackness that spread'? Look at the phrase 'we shall do you' and notice how it includes Ralph and Piggy. Why is this, do you suppose?

■ Self-test questions Chapters 5–8

Uncover the plot
Delete two of the three alternatives given, to find the correct plot. Beware possible misconceptions and muddles

Jack/Piggy/Ralph, burdened by unaccustomed insights into his past/human nature/how to hunt, calls another meeting. As darkness falls, and the boys discuss their fear of Jack/the beast/the parachutist, the assembly disintegrates into chaos. To Roger's/Jack's/Piggy's distress, Ralph considers giving up the leadership/

conch/glasses. An injured parachutist/a rescue party/a dead parachutist drops into the island; Ralph and Jack/Samneric/Roger and Simon, tending the fire, see it and believe that they are about to be rescued/have seen the beast/have seen a ghost. Jack and Ralph lead a search to find the beast, leaving Piggy with the littluns/alone/with the parachutist. The hunt goes on after darkness falls and the group is terrified into flight by the boar/pig/corpse. Ralph/Piggy/Jack calls a meeting and calls Ralph's/Jack's/Roger's leadership into question; when none of the boys respond he leaves, humiliated and enraged. Simon's suggestion that they climb the mountain again is mocked, and he goes to his private place where he falls into a trance/is attacked/dies. At the suggestion of Piggy/Ralph/Simon, the boys light a new fire down on the beach, but the boys gradually defect to Jack's camp. Jack's 'tribe' hunt and kill a pig and leave its ass/head/corpse on a stick as a gift to the beast. In Simon's trance it speaks to him as the Lord of the Flies/Samneric/Bill, as the beast of evil within man.

Who? What? Why? When? Where? How?
1 Walking to the evening meeting, why is Ralph 'overcome with astonishment'?
2 What does Ralph realise about Piggy?
3 What points does Ralph make at the meeting?
4 Why does Simon feel a 'perilous necessity' to speak? What does he think the beast is?
5 Of whom is Piggy scared, and why? What does he say will happen to him (Piggy) if Ralph stands down as chief?
6 According to Simon, where will Ralph get back to?
7 Who joins Ralph and Jack in the 'mad expedition' up the mountain?
8 What does Ralph say about Jack's hunters, and why does Piggy say 'Now you done it.'?
9 What does Ralph mean when he asks Piggy 'what's wrong', and why does he ask Piggy?
10 When Jack and his savages come to steal fire from Ralph's group, how does Jack appear? How does his appearance differ from before?

Who is this?
1 Who 'With a convulsion of the mind, discovered dirt and decay…'?
2 Who 'could think…could go step by step inside that fat head of his'?
3 Who says: '…there isn't no fear, either…unless we get frightened of people'?
4 Who 'At first was a silent effigy of sorrow; but then the lamentation rose out of him, loud and sustained as the conch…'?
5 Who 'became inarticulate in his effort to express humankind's essential illness'?
6 Who 'can't hurt you: but if you stand out of the way he'd hurt the next thing'?
7 Who 'fell and crumpled among the blue flowers of the mountain-side'?
8 Who 'is sitting up there, waiting…and hunting'?
9 Who 'was happy and wore the damp darkness of the forest like his old clothes'?
10 Who said: 'I'm part of you? Close, close, close? I'm the reason why it's no go'?

Facing the fear
Comment on what the following speeches about fear reveal about the speaker.
1 'I'm not talking about the fear. I'm talking about the beast. Be frightened if you like. But as for the beast…' (Jack)
2 'Life…is scientific…I know there isn't no beast – not with claws and all that, I mean – but I know there isn't no fear, either…Unless…we get frightened of people.' (Piggy)
3 'Last night I had a dream, a horrid dream, fighting with things, those twisty things in the trees.' (Phil, a littlun)

4 'If you're scared of someone you hate him but you can't stop thinking about him. You kid yourself he's all right really, an' then when you see him again; it's like asthma an' you can't breathe.' (Piggy)

5 'As long as there's light we're brave enough. But then? And now that thing squats by the fire as though it didn't want us to be rescued...' (Ralph)

Lord of the Flies

Answer the following questions on the important scene at the end of Chapter 8. Remember that there are no simple answers. Golding wants you to think about things on lots of levels. The exploration is as important as arriving at the answer.

1 What is the Lord of the Flies, and what images does the name conjure up?

2 Can you think of any 'religious' parallels to be drawn from Simon's confrontation with the Lord of the Flies? Think carefully about Simon's 'private place', the way in which the hunters present the pig's head, the image of the black mouth.

3 What literal 'reason' could be given for Simon's experience?

4 Why do you think the Lord of the Flies includes Jack in the list of people that Simon likes?

5 What might the Lord of the Flies mean by 'down there' ('You know perfectly well you'll only meet me down there...')?

Chapter 9

Simon sleeps after his conversation with the Lord of the Flies. Storm clouds build up over the island. Still alone, Simon climbs the mountain, and discovers the truth about 'the beast'. He untangles the lines of the parachute so that the figure no longer bows and sits up in the wind. He makes his way down the mountain to tell the others.

All the boys have been attracted to Jack's camp, even Ralph and Piggy. They go partly for the meat and partly out of curiosity. Jack is enthroned as chief and is painted. He is haughty but he invites every boy to join his tribe. Ralph argues with him. A great storm begins. Piggy tries to get Ralph to leave because he thinks there is going to be trouble. Jack urges them all to join in a ritual dance, with Roger miming the roles of pig and hunter. Thunder roars and lightning flashes – just as Simon crawls out of the jungle towards the camp. The dancing, frenzied boys see him as the beast and, shrieking and chanting, they beat him to death, then run for shelter from the storm. Simon's body is carried out to sea by the rising tide.

Simon speaks aloud to the clearing

The beast

How does Simon's question, 'What else is there to do?' show that his confrontation with the Lord of the Flies has not weakened his quest for truth? On what previous occasion has Simon spoken these words? At the summit of the mountain, Simon has seen what 'the beast' really is. It is only a dead man. This incident shows how accurate both Piggy and Simon have been in their understanding that in some way fear comes from inside humans.

'Simon felt his knees smack the rock'

Simon

Simon shows saintly or Christ-like compassion in freeing the parachute's lines. He looks down from the mountain onto the camp. Like Moses in the Bible, Simon will bring the truth down from the mountain only to find that his people have become degenerate and have fallen to worshipping false gods.

'Meanwhile, down on the beach...'

Darkness and death

The approach of darkness and the storm is made to suggest the coming horror. In the light of what is about to happen, notice the irony of Piggy's excuse for going to Jack's feast.

Jack is now 'painted and garlanded', sitting like 'an idol'. What does this tell you about his leadership? In what tone of voice does he speak to his tribe?

'Piggy and Ralph came to the edge...'

Even after the boys have split into two camps, they are united for a moment in making fun of Piggy. Notice all the references at this point to laughter.

What indications are there that Jack rules his tribe by fear? Can you think

Savagery

why Jack has to rule by force and fear? Notice that Jack wishes them to be afraid not of himself, but of a much older enemy: the evil within all humans. Jack wins new followers through a mixture of fear and promises of a higher standard of living (pig meat). How does this parallel history around the time the novel is set?

"Who is going to join my tribe?"

Against the growth of tyranny, the law-abiding population – symbolised by

The conch

Ralph, Piggy and Simon – is helpless. They do not realise until it is too late that Jack's followers have no respect for lawful society.

When Jack invites the others to join his tribe, Ralph replies: 'I'm chief' and says: 'I've got the conch'. How much does the word 'tremulously' tell you about Ralph's position? By asking who wants to have 'fun', is Jack deliberately manipulating the others, or is he simply being irresponsible?

'The dark sky was shattered...'

Savagery

Jack answers Ralph's appeal to sense and logic with the ritual frenzy of the dance. The chant becomes sinister. Compare its words with those of the chant in Chapter 4. Why have they changed? The lightning and the chant whip the tribe into a frenzy. Where are Ralph and Piggy at this stage? Notice Golding's language; the circle of screaming, savage boys has become a single organism – the real beast.

Simon has brought the truth, to release the boys from their fear

Simon is trying to tell the boys about the beast, even whilst he is being

battered to death. Notice the biblical echo of the Crucifixion in the mention of a dead man on a hill.

Those who see the truth of the situation, like Simon, and those who are on the side of what is right and good, like Piggy, are subjected to 'the shrill screaming that rose before the beast'.

Simon

What effect is Golding creating by calling Simon 'the beast' in this scene? The actions of 'the beast' (Simon) are pitifully human, it is still trying to explain the truth. The crowd is like a pack of savage, crazed animals.

> Simon's death is shocking and a significant event for many essay topics. Notice, however, that Golding preserves some element of innocence. The violent storm blurs vision and judgement and Golding presents events from the boys' point of view: in the account of the murder itself Simon is always (with one telling exception) 'the beast'.

Just as Simon dies, the dead parachutist drifts out to sea and vanishes. The words 'Now a great wind…' echo an occasion in a Bible story. What is the significance of this? (Check that part of the Bible which tells what happened when the crucified Jesus died.)

Who is to blame for Simon's death?

Could Simon have done anything to prevent his own death? If the other boys

had listened to him, would they have been saved from savagery? Or does Simon have to die before the boys can be saved? Is this the point of the story of the Crucifixion of Jesus?

The colour imagery used in connection with Simon changes after his death. What is Simon's colour now? Is Piggy correct to reject the use of the word 'murder' in connection

Simon

with Simon's killing? Golding's language makes Simon's death beautiful: 'Somewhere over the darkened curve of the world…'. The sea takes Simon's body 'softly', and merges it with the energies of the natural world. Why is this a fitting end for him?

Chapter 10

Ralph and Piggy are dirty, bruised and covered in shame the next morning. They cannot at first bring themselves to put into words the events of the night. Only Samneric and some littluns now remain with them. Piggy tries to explain how none of them is really to blame for what happened to Simon, but Ralph says bluntly that they took part in a murder.

Jack rules his tribe with beatings and torture. He tells them that the beast was disguised and is not really dead, therefore they must guard their camp. He plans to raid Ralph's camp to get Piggy's glasses. Ralph's small group struggle to keep their fire alight. Ralph finds concentration hard now and at night his previously comforting dream of home becomes a nightmare. Piggy fears they will all lose their sanity. Jack's group attacks, taking Piggy's glasses but leaving the conch. Jack's victory seems complete.

"Call an assembly?"

The conch

Ralph laughs at the suggestion that they should call an assembly. Can you identify the emotion which causes Ralph to laugh? He describes Simon's death as 'murder'. Why does he feel the need to do this? Note that Piggy, the thinker, cannot bring himself to think about the terrible deed: 'We can't do no good thinking about it, see?'

"We was scared!" said Piggy excitedly

This is Piggy's explanation for the ritual killing of Simon. Ralph is searching

Darkness
and death

for a way to explain an entirely different emotion. Can you define this emotion? Ralph reacts to Simon's murder by regressing momentarily into infancy. Piggy tries to convince Ralph that Simon's death was an accident. He uses his poor eyesight to excuse his moral blindness. Why is he being dishonest? How does this fit in with Piggy's usual common sense?

Samneric appear

Savagery

Look at the words 'They flushed and looked past him into the air.' Ralph, Piggy and Samneric are trying to cope with the guilt they feel for taking part in Simon's ritual killing. This is why the word 'dance' is now 'obscene' to them all. What does their guilt tell us about them? Do you think Jack feels guilty?

Over at Castle Rock, Roger returns to the camp

Roger

Why do you think Roger considers Jack to be 'a proper Chief'? What event does this foreshadow? Jack's tyrannical regime allows sadistic actions to take place, like the promised beating of Wilfred (for which we are never given a reason). What parallels can you see with recent world history?

When Roger hears that a littlun is about to be beaten and is possibly being tortured, he responds by 'assimilating the possibilities of irresponsible authority'. What 'possibilities' are there for irresponsible authority that are impossible for responsible authority? What does this tell you about Roger's character?

Jack orders his tribe to defend the gate to their new camp

Jack manipulates the emotions of his followers by suggesting they guard against two dangers. What are the two dangers? Jack presents an 'implication of further terrors' to his tribe – can you think of two reasons why he tells them that they didn't kill the beast after all?

Jack

Back on the beach, Piggy and Ralph light a fire

What does Ralph think the 'double function' of the fire is? The boys are showing clear signs of mental and emotional deterioration. Can you say why Piggy is stronger than Ralph at this point? Ralph's 'nightly game of supposing' tells you about his current state of mind. Why is Ralph's game sad?

Ralph's 'game of supposing' is, of course, not a game at all, but a device to hang on to sanity. Note that he seeks stability in the structures of everyday life (a bus station). It has been the inability to create structures, as well as the violence and evil, that has reduced him to his present state: 'defenceless with the darkness pressing in.'

Ralph dreams of 'lamps and wheels'. These represent man's developed technology, ways in which man has triumphed over distance and darkness. Compare this with the situation on the island.

What does Ralph's uncontrollable laughter tell us about him? Notice how his body 'jumped and twitched'. Compare this with Piggy's 'dignity'. Ralph's game of supposing continues in his sleep, but becomes a nightmare.

Order

'Desperately, Ralph prayed that the beast would prefer littluns.'

Read this section carefully, noting the reactions of Ralph and Piggy. This is the two boys' final consideration of the beast. How has their view of the beast changed since Chapter 1? Notice the way animals are suggested by words 'vicious snarling' and 'biting', and how this changes to blend animals with humans, as with the word 'fingers'. The beast is no longer an unknown animal of some kind, it is human.

The beast

The stealing of Piggy's glasses

The conch

The theft of Piggy's glasses represents the last defeat of the power of reason on the island. Which word suggests that 'the Chief' treats the glasses as a trophy from the hunt? Thieves normally steal what they (or others) value. What is revealed by the fact that the savages did not bother to steal the conch?

Chapter 11

Piggy tells a pathetically small assembly that he must go to Jack to demand his glasses. They set off, Piggy carrying the conch. They draw near to the rock wall of Jack's stronghold on Castle Rock. Ralph shouts at Jack, calling him a thief. Jack orders that the twins be taken captive. Piggy tries to reason with the tribe but as he does so, Roger levers a large rock from higher up. This crashes down, smashes the conch, and hits Piggy – who falls forty feet to his death. The sea takes his body. Ralph escapes as Jack's tribe turn on him. Roger advances to torture the prisoners.

The influence of the conch

At the end of Chapter 10, Ralph's group are pleased to find that the conch

The conch

has not been stolen. Can you think why they still use the conch? The boys' desire to 'smarten up a bit' before confronting the savage tribe shows that they feel the need to show 'we aren't savages really'. At this stage, do you think Ralph's group fully realise the extent of the tribe's degeneration?

The opening of Chapter 11 is a good example of Golding's ability to reveal the schoolboys beneath the savages. The description of the boys' battered faces ('a mask of dried blood', 'the swollen flap of his cheek', Piggy blinded) contrasts with the symbol of civilisation, the conch, and with the attempt to smarten up and concerns about Jack being 'waxy'.

"Piggy! Stop a minute!"

The conch

Piggy is physically helpless without his glasses, but he shows extreme courage in his decision to face Jack and demand what is 'right'. To what extent does Piggy know his own limitations? This distinguishes Piggy as more 'adult' than the other boys. Think about Piggy's strengths and weaknesses. Do the other boys dislike him *only* because he is fat, has asthma and wears glasses?

'They passed the place where the tribe had danced'

Order

The twisted growth in front of Castle Rock symbolises the formidable task which confronts Ralph's group. There is a contrast between the savages, who 'appeared, painted out of recognition' and Ralph's behaviour when he tells them to 'Stop being silly!' How far does Ralph's manner towards the 'savages' mirror that of the naval officer at the end?

Roger

Roger

Roger becomes more irresponsible as this incident unfolds. Think about what the 'source of power' which begins to 'pulse in Roger's body' could be. He feels this growing power as he becomes aware of the vulnerability of the boys on the ledge beneath. Significantly, Piggy is now kneeling.

Ralph demands Piggy's glasses back

Ralph

Ralph responds to Jack's 'Who says?' with 'I say!' He shows great courage when confronting the tribe. How can you tell that his speech will be ineffectual? He uses schoolboy language: 'You aren't playing the game'. However, the group are now savages, no longer schoolboys.

"I said 'grab them!'"

Order

At the moment of their capture, Samneric 'protested out of the heart of civilisation'. How is this explained by what they say? Ralph's temper breaks at this: 'You're a beast and a swine and a bloody, bloody thief!' is another example of schoolboy language, but notice the irony of the words 'beast' and 'swine'.

'Zup!'

Golding uses the onomatopoeic word 'Zup!' to describe Roger's stone-

Roger

throwing. (Onomatopoeic words are those which are invented to resemble the sound of the action or thing that they describe.) How does this word reduce the threat of 'his one hand still on the lever'? Roger's position gives him an unusual view of Ralph and Piggy. The words Golding uses to describe the way Roger sees them have a particular effect. What is this?

Piggy speaks out

Piggy is brave enough to speak out right up to the moment of his death. Ralph adds to Piggy's plea for rational behaviour. 'Which is better,' he says, 'law and

Piggy

rescue' or 'breaking things up?' Ralph has used these last words before (in Chapters 5 and 8) to describe the disintegration of civilised order. Find them, and think about how Ralph's view of life on the island has altered since the beginning of the novel.

Roger kills Piggy and destroys the conch

Roger

Roger experiences 'a sense of delirious abandonment'. This reveals the extent to which Roger has become a mindless savage. Think about Roger's character. What is Golding warning us about when he describes Jack's sadistic and merciless henchman?

The conch

How does the word 'talisman' add to our sadness at the description of the conch in its last moments before it is smashed? The destruction of the fragile conch symbolises how easily democracy can be overthrown.

Notice the colour of the rock onto which Piggy falls. The scene suggests a sacrifice on a primitive altar. Now look at the use of personification in 'the sea breathed again in a long, slow sigh'. How does this affect your response to Piggy's death? There is irony in: 'Piggy, saying nothing, with no time for even a grunt, travelled through the air...'. Why does Golding make Piggy an object to laugh at even at the moment of his death?

Nature

Study the description of Piggy's death and the way his body is washed out to sea. It is cold, hard, impersonal. Compare this with the description of Simon's death. Why did Golding adopt two different approaches to these similar events?

'The hangman's horror clung round him'

The conch and Piggy are destroyed at the same time. This represents the

Savagery

complete destruction of rationality. After Piggy's murder, Ralph is unable to speak: 'no sound came'. This suggests that intelligent communication has broken down. We are witnessing the birth of a new world, based on the call of the beast, in which the most powerful form of communication is the chant. This reverses the way the world begins in the Bible (John I): 'In the beginning was the Word...'

In considering what goes wrong on the island or the role of Jack as leader, it is worth thinking about why Roger emerges as the most terrifying individual. Is there a suggestion that even Jack is not the final stage of violence and destruction, that there are forces of disorder beyond him?

Roger

Roger is no longer restrained by civilised patterns of behaviour (remember in Chapter 4 he found himself unable to throw stones directly at Henry). Samneric are to be 'persuaded' to join Jack's tribe. It is implied that they are tortured. What do you think is the 'nameless authority' which Roger now wields?

Chapter 12

Ralph is wounded and in hiding. At night he moves towards Jack's camp, angrily smashing the skull of the pig's head on the way. Samneric have been put on guard duty and they tell Ralph he is to be hunted down the next day. They give him meat but are too afraid to help further.

Ralph sleeps in the jungle and wakes to the cries of the hunters. He manages to fight them off for a while. Jack orders boulders to be rolled from the top of Castle Rock. These bounce by Ralph, who narrowly escapes. Jack has the area set on fire. Ralph flees as the fire begins to spread across the island. Like a wild animal, Ralph's only thought is to survive. Driven on to the beach, he collapses, exhausted. A naval officer stands in front of him. The officer's crew saw smoke and have come to investigate. The savages stop the hunt instantly – they are silent, including Jack. Ralph, realising that rescue has arrived, and remembering all that has happened, weeps. So do the other boys. The officer looks towards his cruiser anchored in the lagoon, waiting for them to stop.

'Ralph lay in a covert, wondering about his wounds.'

Ralph's acceptance of the reality of life on the island is shown in the words

Ralph

'But really, this was not Bill. This was a savage...' He still has fleeting moments of hope that they are just boys playing a game: he thinks of symbols of normal civilised behaviour like obeying teachers, wearing caps and claiming 'pax' (literally peace, the old-fashioned term for safety in children's games). However, his hope for safety is absurd. What do you understand by the 'indefinable connection between himself and Jack'? How are Ralph and Jack connected?

The Lord of the Flies

Compare Ralph's and Simon's encounters with the Lord of the Flies. Why

The beast

did Ralph feel 'sick fear and rage'? And why is it that the skull 'won't tell'? Although Ralph smashes the skull, its 'grin' grows larger. He cannot wipe out the evil which the skull symbolises.

In realising that he is an 'outcast', Ralph joins Piggy and Simon. Look at the words he uses to explain this. Notice how they echo Piggy's language.

"It's only me. Ralph."

Samneric are enslaved by a 'new and shameful loyalty'. They represent oppressed people, whose only safety lies in joining the stronger group. How do they help, but also betray, Ralph? Why do they eventually betray him? How would you have reacted in their position?

Roger

Samneric tell Ralph about the plan to hunt him down like a pig. What does this hunt suggest about the depths to which the boys have sunk? Notice Roger's part in the torture. Does he seem worse than Jack? It is Roger who has 'sharpened a stick at both ends' in preparation for the Ralph's death. Think about when such a stick was last used.

Animal imagery

Savagery

Look at the imagery which is used to describe Ralph during the final hunt. This develops during the hunt itself until he finally 'bursts' out of the jungle 'screaming, snarling, bloody'. Ralph uses animal tactics to survive the hunt. This hunt, with its line of pursuers, mirrors the child's playground game of 'chain-he' or 'tag'. Why is this echo of a 'game' intensely ironic?

'Now the fire was nearer...'

Ralph's sense of responsibility is illustrated by his comment that the boys are fools, and by his question 'what would they eat tomorrow'?

Simon

When Ralph at last notices that the stick he took from the pig's head 'was sharpened at both ends' he becomes aware of the implications. Will the hunters merely kill him? The pig's head was on the stick. What did the savages do with the rest of the animal? Ralph's inner voice recalls Simon's prophecy. Does he now think Simon was 'batty'?

'Ralph screamed'

Savagery

The idea of the hunt, developed throughout the book, reaches a climax with the manhunt for Ralph. Reduced to an animal, Ralph 'forgot his wounds' and 'became fear'. What has Ralph learned by this point in the novel? Compare the boy who turned a cartwheel on the beach in Chapter 1 with the creature on the beach now.

Beast from water

The images of war – 'revolver', 'submachine gun' and 'cruiser' – remind us that the boys left a war-torn society and will return to the remains of one. The presence of the officer restores a form of civilised law and order. He

Order

comes from the sea, and the conch, symbol of democratic authority, also came from the sea. But the boys thought that the beast came from the sea. What conclusions can you draw from this apparent contradiction?

The island society has produced tyranny and chaos, and the officer's reaction to Ralph is understandably one of 'wary astonishment'. How do you react to the almost magical appearance of the officer at this point in the novel – with relief? Or are you 'wary' too?

Is this a straightforward 'happy ending'? In real life, do you think that 'the cavalry' always arrives just in time, as in films? Or is Golding making a point by ending the novel in this way, rather than in a believable (but unspeakably horrific) way?

"Hullo."

Ralph speaks to the officer shyly, 'squirming a little, conscious of his filthy

Ralph

….appearance'. In the light of the hunt, is this sudden switch of manner convincing? Or would you expect Ralph to react in this way?

Notice the devastating irony of 'Having a war or something?' The officer does not understand the situation. Who do you think knows more about the true nature of human beings – the adult or the dirty 'little boys' in front of him?

'The officer turned back…'

Order

The naval officer is not presented as a character but as a symbol of the civilised, adult world. This raises the matter of the kind of world to which the boys will be taken. Notice the telling way he says 'We'll take you off', not that he'll take them 'home'. The officer sees Jack as 'a little boy', a 'little scarecrow' and a 'kid'. The effect of this is to scale everything down to size.

"Who's boss here?" "I am", said Ralph loudly.

Ralph

From what you have learned about Ralph, why do you think he claims the leadership here? Our final view of Jack is of a 'little boy'. Why do you think Jack decided not to claim the leadership? Piggy's glasses hang as a trophy at Jack's waist. They are a poignant reminder of him, and represent the tribe's loss of reason.

> Considering the novel both as a fictional narrative and as an expression of a view of Mankind, you should decide whether you think that the ending is suitable. How happy an ending is it? Does Golding stop here because any further violence would be excessive and incredible? Is Ralph's survival a sign of hope?

"We saw your smoke."

Ironically the fire, which Ralph once saw as his only possibility of rescue, has at last brought it: but this fire was lit for quite another reason.

The officer's words about 'British boys' being 'able to put up a better show' echo the earlier, civilised standards of the boys. Can you hear the echo of Jack's words: 'After all…We're English' (Chapter 2)? Like the boys at the start of the book, the officer assumes that being civilised and reasonable come naturally. But notice how he also calls them a 'pack'.

Order

"Jolly good show."

The officer refers to a nineteenth-century novel, *Coral Island*. But that novel,

though concerned with a group of stranded boys, is not a study in realism in the way *Lord of the Flies* is. The officer's comment illustrates his ignorance of what has really taken place on the island.

By the end of the novel, fire has destroyed the island.

Darkness and death

Golding implies that the atomic warfare mentioned in Chapter 1 may already have destroyed the rest of the earth. The boys are no more evil, destructive or irresponsible than the adults have been. 'The burning wreckage of the island' illustrates the loss of paradise and the loss of innocence. The fire is an image of blazing hell, from which the children emerge completely changed.

Golding deliberately did not include girls in the novel. He did not want to 'complicate' the fable. What would have happened if girls had also been on the island? Can you imagine the effect on the novel if Ralph, Simon, Piggy, Jack or Roger had been girls? Would the end of the story have been any different?

"Ralph wept for the end of innocence…"

Has Golding ever actually shown the boys as 'innocent'? Seeing the novel as

a fable, Ralph's tears could be caused by the recognition of the fallen nature of all humankind. Innocence can sometimes be confused with plain ignorance. Ralph can no longer see the world as secure, because he has gained knowledge of the evil which lurks in 'the darkness of man's heart'.

Ralph

Why is the officer embarrassed by the boys' tears? Why does Golding present a warship as the final image? What does this imply about the world the boys return to?

The heart of darkness

'The darkness of man's heart' is a reference to *Heart of Darkness*, a short novel by Joseph Conrad, set in the African jungle and dealing with the force of evil, especially within people. What do you think is the 'darkness' which Golding believes is within the heart of all humankind? Now that you have read the novel, try to put an explanation of this 'darkness' into your own words.

■ Self-test questions Chapters 9–12

Uncover the plot

Delete two of the three alternatives given, to find the correct plot. Beware possible misconceptions and muddles.

Simon recovers from his fit and returns to the beach/destroys the Lord of the Flies/climbs the mountain to discover the truth about 'the beast'/the conch/the chief. He sets out to tell the others. Ralph and Piggy break up/join/set fire to Jack's party; as a violent storm breaks, Percival/the littlun with the birthmark/Simon returns and is killed by the dancing, chanting Roger/beast/group. The reign of the Lord of the Flies/Jack/Roger over his tribe becomes increasingly tyrannical/democratic/friendly. After he burns/raids/breaks up Ralph's camp and steals Piggy's glasses/Samneric/the conch, the two/three/four boys go to Castle Rock and demand them back. The twins defect/are killed/are captured, and Roger/Jack/Bill sends a great rock down which kills Piggy and smashes the conch. Ralph breaks down/gives up/escapes. Samneric warn him that Jack intends to hunt him down. A desperate chase follows, during which Ralph/the savages/a naval officer sets fire to the island. The smoke attracts a British cruiser.

Who? What? Where? When? Why? How?
1   Why does Simon free the lines of the parachute from the rock? (9)
2   How does Jack preside over his feast? (Chapter 9)
3   What happens to the dead parachutist? (Chapter 9)
4   How do Ralph, Piggy and the twins react to each other after Simon's murder? (Chapter 10)
5   What was Jack's original reason for raiding Ralph's camp? (Chapter 10)
6   What kind of fire has Jack's tribe lit? (Chapter 11)
7   When does Ralph finally lose his temper? (Chapter 11)
8   When does Ralph think Jack will 'let him alone'? (Chapter 12)
9   How does the naval officer describe the boys' situation? (Chapter 12)
10   Why does Ralph weep? (Chapter 12)

Who is this?
1   Who 'pushed on, staggering sometimes with his weariness but never stopping'?
2   Who 'hung on his stick like a black ball'?
3   Who said: 'I don't ask you to be a sport, I'll say, not because you're strong, but because what's right's right'?

4 Who 'had tied their hair back and were more comfortable than (Ralph) was.'?
5 Who 'protested out of the heart of civilisation'?
6 Who shouts: 'Which is better – to have rules and agree, or to hunt and kill?'
7 Who 'needed a bath, a haircut, a nose-wipe and a good deal of ointment'?
8 Who is the 'little boy who wore the remains of an extraordinary black cap on his red hair and carried the remains of a pair of spectacles at his waist'?

Strip or be stripped
Throughout the action of the novel, characters gradually lose or are forced to give up many things (clothes, morals, possessions, memories). Let's explore.
1 What is stripped from the dead parachutist?
2 What do the boys rob from Simon? Comment on the way in which he dies. What do you think Golding is trying to do in the description of Simon's body being washed out to sea?
3 What two objects does Piggy value? What happens to them? Do they have a significance that goes beyond the literal?
4 What do Jack and Roger take from Samneric?
5 In Chapter 12, what has Ralph lost? What loss hurts him most deeply ('words could not express the dull pain of these things…')?

Fun and games
1 At the beginning of the novel, which books do the boys name as being 'like' their situation? Who else refers to one of these books? What is Golding trying to do when he refers to them?
2 How do the littluns 'play' on the beach in Chapter 4? Is it entirely fun and lighthearted? How does play and fun change throughout the book (give an example)?
3 In Chapter 4, when Jack attacks Piggy and breaks his glasses, what does Ralph say? How does this reflect Ralph's sense of responsibility and fairness? Can you think of any other occasions on which this essentially 'British' awareness of fair play is expressed?
4 How does Golding achieve a new perspective on the situation when the officer comes to rescue the boys? Do you think it is a 'true' perspective, or a misleading one?
5 What is Ralph unable to do? Why do you think Jack does not challenge Ralph's claim to be 'in charge'?

How to write an examination essay

Most of you will be studying *Lord of the Flies* as a set text for your formal examination. This section gives you some guidelines on how to approach an examination essay and also considers three possible subjects.

Before you start writing

- The first essential is thorough revision. It is important that you realise that even Open Book examinations require close textual knowledge. You will have time to look up quotations and references, but *only if you know where to look*.

- Read the questions very carefully, both to choose the best one and to take note of *exactly* what you are asked to do. Do not answer the question you imagine or hope has been set, or repeat the practice essay you wrote earlier on a *similar but slightly different* subject.

- Identify all the key words in the question that mention characters, events and themes, and instructions as to what to do, e.g. compare, contrast, comment, explore, explain, etc. It is very unlikely that simple retelling of the story will gain you much credit.

- Look at each of the points you have identified and jot down what you are going to write about each.

- Decide in what order you are going to deal with the main points. Number them in sequence. This is a matter of choice, but do not use chronological order unless you have a good reason to.

Writing the essay

- The first sentences are important. Try to summarise your response to the question so the examiner has some idea of how you plan to approach it. Do not begin, 'When Ralph calls the boys together by blowing on the conch, Jack leads the choir along the beach in full uniform...' A good beginning on the differences between Ralph and Jack might be, 'Both Ralph and Jack believe in order, but in different types of order. The potential for conflict is present from their first meeting, and gradually their views on society move so far apart that open hostility is inevitable.' Jump straight into your argument; do waste time at the start. A personal response is rewarded, but you must always answer the question: as you write your essay, *refer back to your list of points*.

- Answer *all* of the question. Many students spend all their time answering just one part of a question and ignoring the rest. This prevents you gaining marks for the parts left out. In the same way, failing to answer enough questions on the examination is a waste of marks which can always be gained most easily at the start of an answer.

- There is no 'correct' length for an essay. What you must do is to spend the full time usefully in answering all parts of the question (spending longer than the allocated time by more than a few minutes is dangerous). Some people write faster than others, but they don't always get the best marks!

- Take care with presentation, spelling and punctuation. It is generally unwise to use slang or contractions (e.g. 'they've' for 'they have').

- Use quotation or paraphrase when it is relevant and contributes to the quality and clarity of your answer. References to events often do not need quotation, but the exact words of such things as the tribe's chants or Simon's communications with the Lord of the Flies would be valuable. *Extended quotations* are usually unhelpful and are often used as padding, which is a complete waste of time.

Example questions

Below are three examples of the kind of questions you may expect in your exam. An *outline* of a model answer has been supplied for each question. You will find it useful to write full-length versions of these plans, incorporating references from the text to back up the ideas.

1 *Although the reader's sympathies are usually with Ralph, many of the boys decide to follow Jack. Explain what you think are the differences in what Ralph and Jack stand for and in how they behave in the novel.* (NEAB specimen question)

- To obtain information for this title in the Guide, you will find the section on **Order** in **Themes** particularly helpful, plus, of course, the sections on the two boys and many parts of the **Text commentary**.

- The first stage in answering this is to identify the task precisely. You are *not* asked to explain why we sympathise with Ralph or why the boys follow Jack, though reference to these points will doubtless occur incidentally. You *are* asked to explain (give reasons for/make sense of) the differences in the principles and behaviour of the two boys.

- It might be as well to start with background. Ralph comes from a comfortable background, is perhaps brought up to become a leader, but despite his father's life in the services, nothing has happened to destroy his basic mildness. Jack is associated with a world of rules and uniforms. He has been given too much authority for one so young: not quite of life and death, but it is he who decides whether the fainting Simon is to receive attention. The uniforms obliterate the individual, just as warpaint will do, more dangerously.

- From this you can deduce an essential difference in what the two boys believe about order. Both know it is essential, but their versions take different forms and have different goals. Jack wishes to impose order, to punish wrongdoers, to emphasise ritual, to lead as 'chief': his policies have short-term advantages (food), but no long-term objectives. Ralph wishes order to be agreed democratically via a series of rules, the conch being a symbol of democracy and the right to free speech (just like the British boys whom the naval officer expects to find behaving themselves). He has a long-term objective (rescue) which means giving up present delights for the boring routine of fire-duty.

- If you wish to explain the appeal of Jack at this point, it should not be difficult: to begin with, he offers more fun and more food, and later his fierce authority prevents desertion.

- Explaining how Ralph and Jack behave in the novel is very straightforward once you have explained the differences in their original principles. They respond to various changes and opportunities during the novel, but essentially act in accordance with their original principles. Jack's assertion of independence and establishment of a cruel tribal dictatorship is gradual, of course, but that is inevitable in the changing situations of the novel. It is possible in the earlier stages (thanks to Ralph's diplomacy) for both boys to believe that they are at the same time working together and carrying out their own agendas. When the issue is forced, Ralph and Jack act in accordance with their behaviour from the very beginning.

- You will find it helpful to consider the skill with which Golding presents his characters as, simultaneously, tribesmen/beleaguered democrats and small boys. Jack deciding not to 'play any longer' when Ralph is re-elected is in accordance with his reaction to not being chosen chief in the first place. Ralph's childhood memories are an important part of his attempts to remain sane and reasonable.

- It is always possible to end an essay by summarising the points you have made and this would be suitable here. If you want a different approach, you could finish by explaining what Jack and Ralph mean in the context of world politics: totalitarian dictatorship versus democracy and all that this involves.

2 *Explain what went wrong on the island and why, in order to bring out what you think Golding has to say about how societies operate.* (NEAB specimen question)

- This is a straightforward question, but not quite as straightforward as it looks. There is something of an invitation to narration ('what went wrong') and your task will, in part, be to deal with the narrative element without letting it dominate.

- Perhaps the best way to consider this title, bearing in mind that you must *explain*, is to divide up the different ways in which things 'went wrong'. There will obviously be a large section on the descent into savagery by Jack and the choir/tribe. Try to bring out the various stages by which early temptations to savagery, as in Jack's failure to attack the pig, and early signs of almost military discipline, like the choir's first appearance, gradually merge to produce a violent and murderous tribe.

- You must not, however, place all responsibility on Jack and the tribe. Ralph and Piggy favour a system which requires a civilised and orderly society, but you will find no trouble in charting the collapse of the infrastructure of this society. Most of the huts do not even reach completion, it is arguable whether the fire would have been maintained even without the desertion of the hunters (Jack's volunteering them makes for a convenient scapegoat), there is no adequate provision for food, hygiene or checking of numbers, etc. Society is undermined as much by fear as by violence: would terror of the 'enemy' (the beast) have increased or decreased without Jack's hunters?

- At the time of writing this book, Golding had limited faith in human nature and it shows in the reasons why everything went wrong. Think of the ways in which the boys succumb to temptation in deserting Ralph for the glamorous and well-fed life of a hunter.

- Equally important as explaining how things deteriorated is assessing what Golding is saying about how societies operate. There are several different angles from which you could approach this. The warning against Fascist-style dictatorships is the most obvious: note that Golding is fair in presenting the appeal of the grandiose speeches, the uniforms, the triumphs, etc, as well as the essential evil. What is he saying about democracy? Probably that democracy cannot exist simply on rules/laws and a few symbols (the conch, in this case); it relies also on the good will, understanding and security of the people. He also suggests various other unappealing ways in which societies work. The weak are oppressed; the outsider (e.g. Simon) is feared, mocked or persecuted; hypocrisy and dishonesty about motives are commonplace; material comfort (in this case, food) has more impact than ideals, etc.

- Probably a good way to conclude this essay would be to put the various elements together to explain why *Lord of the Flies* is such a pessimistic book. Golding manages simultaneously to stress both that democracy and ideals are vital and that human failings make them unachievable.

3 *How far do the characters of* Lord of the Flies *continue to reflect the behaviour and social background of their lives in England? Which of them are most changed by their lives on the island and which remain closest to their original personalities?*

- The first point that needs to be made is that most of the boys are drastically changed, yet never leave behind their original characters. The great success of *Lord of the Flies* (very difficult to reproduce on film) is to present characters who are *simultaneously* savages and English schoolboys. Ralph, for instance, having fled the tribe as a hunted animal, greets the naval officer with a shy 'Hullo' and worries about his appearance. Jack and the tribe, pursuing Ralph through ferns and undergrowth, sound like a group of boys playing Cowboys and Indians: it is not even unusual to light fires in play, though not with such deadly intent! If we examine the various characters, we will find many vestiges of a former life.

- There are various ways of approaching this title. The most obvious (and a perfectly good way of tackling it) is to consider one character at a time. A different possibility is to consider various themes as they apply to a number of characters. The theme of social class could be particularly rewarding. Ralph, despite his mildness of temperament, is a member of the 'officer class'. How does this affect the assumptions he makes and the ways others treat him? The officer's brief conversation makes all sorts of assumptions as to the type of boy Ralph is. Remember that traditional class divisions were much stronger in the 1950s than now. Why is it that Piggy, for all his intelligence, is not seen as a leader or even as a serious figure? One of the reasons (by no means the only one) is an accent and view of life reminiscent of the corner sweet-shop. (It is, incidentally, surprising how little presence the working and lower-middle classes have in this book.) Jack benefits very strongly from the hierarchies of the English education system.

- The survival of traces from another life could be explored across different examples, starting, probably, from Percival Wemys Madison who eventually loses touch with the talisman of civilisation. You can find Jack refusing to play any more when the vote goes against him or Samneric, very late in the book, worrying about Jack becoming 'waxy' (like their least favourite teacher). Look at all the speech in the confrontation between Jack and Ralph in Chapter 11 and you may feel that the slang reflects an old-fashioned playground more than Castle Rock.

- Then you need to turn to considering who changes most and least. This is a matter of opinion, though it needs to be backed by evidence. Ralph and Piggy, for instance, change little essentially, though learning and being shaped by circumstance. How much does Jack change? A choirboy and a tribal chief are far-distant ways of life, but perhaps his essential character in revealed at the outset, in his attitude to such things as Simon fainting and the issue of choosing a chief. The visionary powers of Simon constitute a major change, but what about Roger as the most changed character? Even here, it is a character revealed and developed, rather than transformed: look, for instance, at the hints in Chapter 4.

- A neat conclusion to the essay might be that the process of change is less total than you might expect because of what Golding believes about the sinfulness of Man and his jaundiced understanding of the world of small boys.

■ How to write a coursework essay

Most of you are unlikely to write a coursework essay on *Lord of the Flies* as such, but you might wish to use the book as the twentieth-century comparison to pre-twentieth-century fiction in a Wide Reading assignment. If you do so, you should bear in mind the following points.

- There must be a *specific* ground for comparison. The comparison should be made throughout the essay, not necessarily in the same sentence, but at least in adjacent paragraphs.

- You can use *Lord of the Flies* with a very different novel or short story, but there must be one definite respect (or more than one) in which you can find similarities or differences or both.

- For example, if you are writing on a Charles Dickens novel like *Oliver Twist* or *Great Expectations*, the plots will bear no resemblance to each other, but you will find much material on the presentation of childhood. Dickens' view of childhood is almost opposite to Golding's. His young people are idealised, they learn from sufferings and develop an acute moral sense, and his treatment of them, though often amusing and convincing, always has a sentimental element. Golding's view of original sin and the shallowness of civilisation is a perfect contrast. You are also aided by the fact that Dickens writes mainly of boys, as does Golding, though Dickens' creations are often projections of his own character.

- There are nineteenth-century novels which have a direct link to *Lord of the Flies*, notably *The Coral Island*. *Lord of the Flies* can almost be seen as a commentary on R M Ballantyne's book (there are even name similarities), but unfortunately *The Coral Island* is not an acceptable text for pre-twentieth-century fiction.

- Apart from novels about childhood (Dickens is the best, but not the only, choice), you could compare *Lord of the Flies* with a novel that criticises Man and society by an account of another distant land. *Gulliver's Travels* is a book for which *Lord of the Flies* could provide a relevant comparison. The difference in plot is that Gulliver is ship wrecked into lands where society already exists; the difference in tone is that, though Swift's humour is barbed, bitter and satirical, it is nonetheless humour. You will find comparisons worth making in the shared disgust at Mankind and the different ways of revealing it.

- A more eccentric choice, but still possible, is Mary Shelley's *Frankenstein*. The progress from optimism to despair, the unexpected creation of an uncontrollable monster, are there in both, plus some oblique views on the power of science.

- It is essential to make reference to the historical, social and cultural background of the texts. This will not be a problem with *Lord of the Flies*. The novel belongs clearly to the Cold War/atom bomb/arms race period in the aftermath of the Second World War and, in a less dramatic way, the boys' clothing, manners and speech place the novel is a recognisable period and society. Both of these would need to be explained in an essay.

With any coursework essay (whether a comparison or a study of one text) there are certain considerations always to be borne in mind:

- It is essential that you show considerable evidence of textual knowledge, even if the essay has a strong creative element.

- In an analytical essay the *most important* consideration is that you must develop an argument or explain a point of view throughout. Careful advance preparation will aid you in organising your theme or argument: making notes on the material, putting these notes in order, then working through two or three drafts of the essay. In this way you should be able to make a decision on what each paragraph is about, as far as possible signalling this to the reader in the opening sentence, often called a *topic sentence* because it states the topic of the paragraph.

- If you are writing an imaginative/creative essay, the *first essential* is to reveal throughout your factual knowledge of the text and a soundly based interpretation of it. Mere imagination will not gain credit in textual study for GCSE English Literature.

- In terms of length of essay, do bear in mind that it is only one of several pieces of coursework and there is no need for a 5,000 word blockbuster. Many essays will exceed 1,000 words; by how much you write depends on the material you wish to present and the advice of your teacher.

Self-test answers Chapters 1–4

Uncover the plot

While evacuating children from a war zone, a plane crashes on a remote tropical island. Two young boys, Ralph and Piggy, meet up and Ralph blows a conch shell to gather up the rest of the survivors. The group of boys elect Ralph as their leader; this annoys Jack, the confident leader of the choir, but he is appeased when Ralph volunteers the choir as hunters. Ralph, Jack and Simon explore the island and find it uninhabited. Another meeting is called, at which it is decided that the conch should give the person holding it the right to speak; some of the smaller ones describe their fear of a 'beastie' that comes out of the jungle at night. The group starts a signal fire using Piggy's glasses, which rages out of control and kills one of the littluns. Jack learns to hunt pigs, while Ralph struggles to get the other boys to help build shelters. Jack paints his face and takes the choir, who are supposed to be tending the fire, on a hunt. The fire goes out and a ship passes in the distance. There is a tense confrontation when the hunters return, during which Jack attacks Piggy and breaks his glasses. Matters are partially resolved as they roast and eat the pig, and Ralph calls another meeting.

Who? What? Why? Where? When? How?

1 That there are no grown-ups on the island; Jack says '…then we'll all have to look after ourselves'
2 Call him by his former nickname, Piggy
3 For his stillness, his size, his attractive appearance, and because he possesses the conch
4 They all rush forward and Jack raises his knife, but he cannot bring himself to commit the 'enormity' of hurting a living creature
5 The compulsion to track down and kill
6 To a hideaway in the jungle
7 Eating and playing on the beach
8 A taboo of civilisation remaining from the old life – the invisible protection of parents, school, policemen and the law
9 Bill is frightened by the savagery in Jack's eyes
10 Simon; perhaps because he has shown compassion, therefore laying himself open to mockery and showing himself different from 'the group'

Who is this?

1 Ralph
2 Piggy
3 Jack
4 According to Jack, Simon
5 Roger
6 Jack
7 Simon
8 Piggy

Creative colour

1 The description of the conch shell emphasises its purity and beauty, but also its delicacy. The conch becomes a symbol of order and democracy, representing the civilised ideal; the action of the novel shows this to be as fragile as the conch itself.
2 Ralph enjoys being naked, until Piggy points out that they might never be rescued. Ralph's shirt then forms a comforting link with his old life, which he

might have lost forever. The grey of the uniform contrasts with the 'natural' colours of the island, such as the blue of the sea and the pink of the rock: perhaps it represents civilisation (and by implication law and order) as opposed to the wildness of nature

3   The black uniform of the choir boys is described as 'strangely eccentric', and it contrasts with the mixture of colours of the other uniforms (fawn, blue, grey) and with the natural colours of the scenery. Black is traditionally associated with evil and darkness, and here it creates a sense of harsh discipline and even of something sinister. Jack's hair is red; does this suggest a fiery temper? When Jack paints his face he uses black, red and white to become an 'awesome stranger' – what else is traditionally associated with the colour red?

4   When Jack first appears on the beach his eyes are 'ready to turn to anger'. Here, their striking, piercing blue emphasises his fierceness and cruelty as the hunt possesses him. Remember that Ralph's eyes are 'mild'. Later in the book Jack's eyes are 'opaque' and 'mad'

5   It is Simon who names the 'candle buds', reacting to their almost spiritual beauty. Like the conch, they are cream and white – beautiful but fragile. Notice the boys' comments: Ralph comments on their beauty ('You couldn't light them… They look just like candles'); Jack, slashing at them with his knife, is contemptuous ('we can't eat them'). It is significant that Simon comes to be alone amidst their scent

Follow my leader

1   He generates obedience through harshness and respect through fear. He has an air of arrogance and superiority. He shows a lack of compassion towards the boys, who are hot and tired, and especially towards Simon who he dismisses as 'always throwing a faint'

2   Merridew (his surname); he says that first names are 'kids' names', and perhaps feels that he will lose some authority if he allows himself to be called by his

3   Because he is leader of the choir and head boy, and because he can sing C sharp. Jack tries to translate his authority at school to authority on the island, and it seems amusingly inadequate. Ralph reacts generously, by offering Jack an important role in charge of the choir/hunters

4   Piggy senses the good in Ralph and the bad in Jack, he is 'timid' before Jack's arrogance. He has an intuitive knowledge of people (see the end of Chapter 5) so that his glasses become a symbol of his clear-sighted common sense

5   Ralph refuses to move from the site of the old fire, so Jack and his group have to build a new fire in a less convenient place. Note how the two boys frequently fail to understand their feelings towards each other, or to express them ('They walked along, two continents of experience and feeling, unable to communicate')

■ Self-test answers Chapters 5–8

Uncover the plot

Ralph, burdened by unaccustomed insights into human nature, calls another meeting. As darkness falls, and the boys discuss their fear of the beast, the assembly disintegrates into chaos. To Piggy's distress, Ralph considers giving up the leadership. A dead parachutist drops into the island; Samneric, tending the fire, see it and believe that they have seen the beast. Jack and Ralph lead a hunt to find the beast, leaving Piggy with the littluns. The hunt goes on after darkness falls and the group is terrified into flight by the corpse. Jack calls a meeting and calls Ralph's leadership into question; when none of the boys respond he leaves, humiliated and enraged. Simon's suggestion that they climb the mountain again is mocked, and he goes to his private place where he falls into a trance. At the suggestion of Piggy, the boys light a new fire down on the beach, but the boys gradually defect to Jack's camp. Jack's 'tribe' hunt and kill a pig and leave its head on a stick as a gift to the beast. In Simon's trance it speaks to him as the Lord of the Flies, as the beast of evil within man.

Who? What? Why? When? Where? How?

1 He is astonished by a sudden 'strange mood of speculation'
2 He realises that Piggy has brains and can think
3 That the coconut shells should have been filled with water; the shelters are inadequate; the boys are no longer using the rocks as a lavatory as agreed; that the fire should never go out, and never be taken from the mountain; and that they should talk about their fears
4 He feels he must explain his conviction that the beast is a part of them, the evil in human nature
5 Of Jack, because he understands Jack's true nature and hatred of Piggy. If Ralph stands down, Jack will hurt Piggy
6 To 'where he came from'
7 Roger
8 That they are 'boys armed with sticks'. Hunting is Jack's 'trade', his obsession; by insulting his hunters Ralph is striking at what Jack holds most dear
9 He means 'why is everything going wrong, and breaking up'; with Ralph's new-found understanding he respects Piggy's brains and intuition
10 Jack is 'stark naked' apart from his paint and his belt. He has now discarded even the ragged shorts that he wore previously

Who is this?

1 Ralph (Chapter 5)
2 Piggy (Chapter 5)
3 Piggy (Chapter 5)
4 Percival (Chapter 5)
5 Simon (Chapter 5)
6 Jack (Chapter 5)
7 The dead parachutist (Chapter 6)
8 The 'beast' (Chapter 8)
9 Jack (Chapter 8)
10 The Lord of the Flies (Chapter 8)

Facing the fear

1 Jack separates the fear from the beast. It does not occur to him that the beast might be something inside himself, causing the fear; for him, the beast is something he can hunt and kill. He has no compassion for those who let fear dominate them
2 Piggy dismisses the 'physical' beast – the monster of our childhood fears – because he believes in the logic of science; he has the insight to recognise that there may be something to fear in human nature
3 Phil describes the nightmare and the fear shared by all the littluns. They believe in a 'snake-beast'. Such physical representations of fear – the beast from the air, the beast from the water – allow the boys to believe that the evil exists outside themselves, and so to believe that they themselves are good
4 Piggy's fear of Jack is justified. He knows that he himself is weak and disadvantaged, and therefore the focus of all Jack's hatred and cruelty; this shows great perception

5　Ralph recognises the power of the darkness to create and magnify fear. His own worst fear – that they will not be rescued – is shown up in his image of the beast sitting up on the mountain

Lord of the Flies

1　Literally, a pig's head on a stick. (Golding, not Simon, gives it this name.) It conjures up images of the devil, evil, death, decay and destruction; it also creates a sense of power (Lord of…)

2　Simon's private place is a kind of church where he goes to be alone and contemplate (remember the candle buds). The hunters present their prize as if they were offering up a sacrifice to appease a cruel god. The black mouth is like hell. Some interpretations see the confrontation of Simon and the Lord of the Flies as good against evil, with evil trying to tempt Simon to join its ranks

3　Simon has a history of fainting fits. The blood that comes from his nose could signify an epileptic fit, during which he experiences nightmarish visions. The whole scene could be seen as an hallucination

4　Simon is shown as having a generosity of spirit and an understanding that allows him to see the good in everyone, even Jack. Can you see anything good in Jack? Or perhaps the Lord of the Flies is trying to tempt Simon into alliance with Jack (with evil) and to persuade him that there is no point resisting such a strong force.

5　'Down there' could mean down in the darkness of unconsciousness into which Simon is falling, or it could mean hell, or it could mean down the mountain where all the boys are congregated. Perhaps, for Simon, down the mountain has come to represent hell

■ Self-test answers Chapters 9–12

Uncover the plot

Simon recovers from his fit and climbs the mountain to discover the truth about 'the beast'. He sets out to tell the others. Ralph and Piggy join Jack's party; as a violent storm breaks, Simon returns and is killed by the dancing, chanting group. The reign of Jack over his tribe becomes increasingly tyrannical. After he raids Ralph's camp and steals Piggy's glasses, the four boys go to Castle Rock and demand them back. The twins are captured, and Roger sends a great rock down which kills Piggy and smashes the conch. Ralph escapes. Samneric warn him that Jack intends to hunt him down. A desperate chase follows, during which the savages set fire to the island. The smoke attracts a British cruiser.

Who? What? Where? When? Why? How?

1　To release the dead man from the indignity of being pulled about by the wind
2　Painted and garlanded, 'like an idol'
3　The wind lifts him and carries him out to sea
4　They find it hard to face each other, or to admit that they were even there
5　To 'steal' fire
6　A cooking fire, not a signal fire
7　When Jack orders his tribe to capture the twins
8　Never
9　'Fun and games'
10　Golding says he weeps for 'the end of innocence, the darkness of man's heart, and the fall through the air of the true, wise friend called Piggy'.

Who is this?

1 Simon (Chapter 9)
2 Lord of the Flies (Chapter 9)
3 Piggy (Chapter 11)
4 Jack's 'savages' (Chapter 11)
5 Samneric (Chapter 11)
6 Piggy (Chapter 11)
7 Ralph, according to the naval officer (Chapter 12)
8 Jack (Chapter 12)

Strip or be stripped

1 Dignity. Does Piggy die in a dignified way?
2 Life. He dies violently, all the time trying to communicate the truth to his attackers. Perhaps a parallel can be drawn with Crucifixion: do the boys 'know what they are doing'? Simon's body is washed gently out to sea (not sucked, like Piggy's); the description is delicate and full of light. Think about what else is pure, white and bright in the book. Is it a coincidence that both Simon's body and that of the parachutist he has 'liberated' go out to sea?
3 His glasses and the conch. His glasses are broken and then stolen; the conch is smashed. His glasses allow him to see, and the boys to have fire. Does Piggy 'see' more clearly than the others? Does he readjust his 'vision' of what is happening on the island? Piggy values the 'talisman' that is the conch, not only because it represents law and democracy but also because he needs it if he is to speak and be heard
4 Their liberty and their right to choose. The twins are intimidated into joining Jack's tribe
5 Ralph has lost Piggy and Simon. He is an outcast and seeks out Samneric for reassurance. At the end of the novel, Ralph weeps for the loss of innocence

Fun and games

1 *Treasure Island*, *Swallows and Amazons* and *Coral Island*. The naval officer ('Like the Coral Island.') The references to lighthearted adventure stories create an ironic parallel with the horror of the boys' real experiences on the island
2 The littluns use play as a way of filling time and distracting themselves from their fears (they cling to the civilisation they have lost by building castles, walls, tracks). Their play is described as 'aimless and trivial'; they find it difficult to adjust to their situation. 'Play' becomes unrestrained and irresponsible, until ritual, chant, dance and superstition allow the boys to torture and to kill. Think about the rock that 'challenges' them in their exploration of the island in Chapter 1; then think about Piggy's death, and the rock that is aimed at Ralph in Chapter 12
3 'That was a dirty trick.' Ralph has a highly developed sense of what is right and fair (he has a strong 'moral' awareness), and objects to Jack taking advantage of Piggy's weakness. Think of the twins' reaction when they are captured in Chapter 11; of the 'schoolmaster' voice of the Lord of the Flies as it 'speaks' to Simon; of Ralph's talk of 'pax' when he is outcast in Chapter 12; and of the officer's talk of 'Jolly good show'. All of these point to the inadequacy of such values before the powerful forces of evil released on the island
4 The naval officer scales the boys down in size (they are 'little'); he reduces the seriousness of their situation by using words like 'ointment', 'nose-wipe' and 'kid'. Perhaps it is a fair representation of how a grown-up – especially a British military man – would assess the situation. For the reader, knowing all that has happened, it is terribly inadequate
5 He can't explain what has happened. Just as Ralph cannot express himself, Jack is unable to assert his chieftainship in the face of this new authority